Life Temporarily Interrupted

*Her Kidneys Failed;
She Didn't Quit*

PATSY BLADES

Life Temporarily Interrupted
Copyright © 2017 by Patsy Blades
All rights reserved

ISBN #__1546836004_____

This book is dedicated to my mother,
Lessie for her never ending support
when I was ill, and my sister,
Sandra for her kindness.
Their selflessness will
never be forgotten.

Table of Contents

Foreword

Life Temporarily Interrupted

*F*acing kidney disease and kidney transplant is complex and often daunting despite the supportive family, staff, and resources available. This book offers an inspiring insight into the author's life adventure successfully dealing with and living through and beyond her kidney transplant. The challenge will have its ups and downs, and this she honestly shares, advising up front that each patient's story is unique, so hopefully the reader's story will have more of the ups she shares than the downs that are unique to her own story. But keep in mind as you read about much of her missteps that her kidney story takes us back to the early days of transplantation, from being sick in 1970 to her kidney transplant in 1976, forty years ago. There has been much learned and much progress made in the four decades since, resulting in fewer of the issues she shares from those early days, but the message of survival is still timely today, and that is the power in reading her amazing story.

As a heart transplant recipient myself, now out 23 years (receiving my 'new' heart back in 1994) who has mentored literally hundreds of transplant candidates and later, the same patients now as transplant recipients, I can recognize many of her experiences as being all too common although not together in any one patient's experience. That's why she gets to write an interesting and inspiring personal story, for who would find the reading of value if it weren't that complex, meaning 'interesting'. Take her advice and don't come away concerned about your own experience having the full array of challenges, but be aware that this isn't a road for the faint of heart. Take consolation in the fact that hundreds of thousands have gone before you and today lead lives that are too normal to warrant writing a book as the author has. How bad can it be if over 85,000 people opt to list and thus get in line here in the U.S. alone this year of 2017 for the opportunity to receive their kidney transplant, hoping for a return to a healthy life lived with energy and passion. While a transplant isn't a 'cure', it offers the hope of a long, fulfilled life and thus the daily challenge of what to do with that gift of life today and the many days, months, and hopefully years that follow. In the closing chapters, Patsy too briefly summarizes her life today, sharing the many blessings that have resulted from her donated kidney, built on a strong faith in God's goodness and her positive outlook so different than throughout her early story years. And, of course, in living more years with the aging process, as she shares in her summary so well, there are other life challenges to deal with, both post-transplant related as well as just general health issues that too often we all have to face if we live long enough.

The author includes a factual and easy to understand medical education, with her gift of language she uses to great effect. But more importantly, she gifts us through her sharing of personal struggles and survival, the inspiration that families and patients need to face and move past their current issues with that positive outlook that often helps to improve the outcome of success we so wish for each day.

The author's life story gives testimony to the value of registering today to be an organ donor after death and/or to be a living donor of a kidney (or donating a partial liver or a single lung) that can be lifesaving or life enhancing to a desperate and suffering fellow human. Come and face your own unique medical challenges with the blessing of not having to undergo all that Patsy has, but with the survival instinct that she shares as a hope for living the life of a true survivor as she has in this beautiful book of life.

Jim Gleason
Heart transplant survivor since 1994

President, TRIO
(Transplant Recipients International Organization)

Author: *A Gift of the Heart* (available free online)

Nationally known speaker and advocate for organ donation

Introduction

*T*his is a true story about my encounter with kidney disease, a condition in which the small blood vessels of the kidneys are damaged, making the organs incapable of functioning normally. They lose their ability to help filter and remove waste products and toxins from the blood and to control the level of fluid in the body. This leads to harmful substances building up in the body and poisoning it. If the problem is ignored, it will eventually lead to sickness and death.

The two most common causes of kidney disease are diabetes and high blood pressure. Other risk factors are heart disease and a family history of kidney failure. Diabetes is a condition in which the body does not efficiently process food for use as energy, which causes high blood-sugar levels. High blood pressure, also known as hypertension, is a condition in which the force of the blood flowing through the arteries is elevated, which can lead to heart disease. One of the heart's jobs is to push the blood through the kidneys for adequate filtering.

My kidney disease did not originate from any of these causes. I did not have diabetes, high blood pressure, or heart problems, and no one in my family history had experienced kidney disease, as far as I am aware. I didn't know until I was diagnosed that kidney disease was a possibility for me, and I never imagined that it could have led to my death.

I immigrated to what I envisioned was a vast and progressive foreign country, the United States of America, in 1969. Within a few weeks, my life had turned upside down. My body reacted to a standard penicillin injection, which resulted in renal failure, sometimes referred to as "end-stage" kidney disease. I was ill prepared to battle the sudden life-threatening crisis that confronted me. My life suddenly shifted from a healthy youth with a promising future full of expectations to a life full of dreams that were put on hold.

This book catalogs the many obstacles I faced, including having to fight for survival, living through scary dialysis treatments, spending long periods in the hospital, and realizing I was a candidate for a kidney transplant. It also includes a poem about the day I received a call that told me I had been given the ultimate gift for someone in my situation — a new kidney.

You will read how the transplant changed my life in a positive way, why I got the surgery, how I survived the process of the transplant itself, how I came to terms with the idea of a transplanted organ in my body, and how I learned to care for this great gift. I have written about my life after surgery and my maintaining hope, which I believe is an important factor for people in a similar predicament to learn and understand.

Part of my story reveals my revised aspirations and career goals after the surgery, particularly the challenge of getting back on my feet and moving forward. I didn't realize at the time that a transplant could lead to more challenges and could require further changes to my lifestyle. This book concludes with a summary of my life and offers words of encouragement followed by a list of kidney and organ transplant movies.

I recommend that anyone who has a friend or loved one waiting for a transplant watch as many related movies as possible to get an idea of what could happen and how to deal with it.

These statements are my personal experiences. I encourage readers to contact local specialists for more information during their research.

A nurse took me to a small room to get undressed, gave me a hospital gown, and instructed me to position the opening at the back. Cold and alone, I sat in the only chair in the room. I thought I would receive a list of precautions and the process I would go through, how long I would be in surgery, and what I might experience. I got none of these things. In hindsight, I should have asked, but the naiveté of youth prevailed. Even if the nurse had given me an instruction sheet, looking at it would have done me little or no good as I was having trouble focusing. After a while, I lay down on the bed and stared at the wall, waiting for the nurse to return. The surgeon entered briefly to introduce himself and then left to prepare for surgery.

I knew I would be unconscious within thirty minutes, under heavy anesthetic, going under the knife, and my life would be in the hands of my urologist. I curled into a fetal position, shivering. All the fears that prevail when anyone has to undergo surgery came to the fore: I would have no say in what happens, no way to save myself if something went wrong, and no way to even know if something went wrong. I simply wouldn't wake up.

In an attempt to rid my mind of these morbid thoughts, I focused on the reason behind the experience. If all went well — no, *when* all went well — I would leave the hospital with a chance at having a life. My health issues would be solved, at least the most critical one. My body would support itself, and I could resume living a healthy, normal life. I would rejoice to know that I have a well-functioning kidney! I would be healthy and fully functional for the first time in years, since my kidneys quit on me. This surgery was the only hurdle standing between my current reality and a healthy future. It was what I needed, and I continually forced myself to keep that thought uppermost in my mind. I closed my eyes and straightened my spine in anticipation of the surgery I had long awaited. It was finally here.

An orderly came into the room, glanced at me, and smiled. With a soft voice he said, "I'm here to take you to the OR (operating room)."

I nodded, and my eyes unfocused. The less I thought about it, the better. I told myself, *It's time to get it over with!* I moved over to the stretcher and the orderly pushed it out the door with the rails up.

An IV (intravenous) nurse came to the room and inserted a tube in my arm. "You will feel a slight pinch — you know the drill." Her voice was comforting. I acknowledged her words with a nod, but when I felt the needle slide into my arm, I held my breath. I had probably felt the sensation a million times before, but I still hadn't learned to ignore the uncomfortable pinch. Thankfully it was over in a few minutes and we were on our way. The orderly wheeled me into the surgical room while I was still wide-awake. I was glad I had gotten the chance to say goodbye to my mother who was always at my side.

It had been years since my first surgery, but I still wasn't accustomed to the wide range of scalpels, needles, and bone saws. I was hoping not to see the tools and equipment of the trade, as that would surely lead to nightmares during the surgery. This was the first time the thought flashed across my brain, *Are nightmares during surgery possible? If they are, can they affect the success of the operation?* I gave myself a mental slap and closed my eyes. There was no point in thinking about those questions. I preferred to have a blank mind, if at all possible.

The anesthesiologist was waiting for me in the surgical room and injected more medication into the IV when I arrived. I felt it traveling up my arm, making my fingers and my arm numb. Before I knew it, my abdomen had followed. Even with this numbing, I was still awake and I glanced at the anesthesiologist in dismay.

"Nothing to worry about; you'll wake up in a couple of hours, and it will be all over." His voice faded toward the end of his sentence as the medication traveled up my neck and into my face and head. My eyes grew heavier, and I closed them and tried to relax. I could hear voices but I tuned them out, turning my thoughts inward. As I slid toward sleep, my mind grew fuzzy and dark. My subconscious took over, and it led me back to where it all began — a time when I was healthy and active.

Chapter 1

Becoming Ill

$\mathcal{A}$s a teenager, I left my native Caribbean Island of Barbados to reside in the United States of America. A few months after I arrived, the shine had worn off my new life and the future was looking somewhat bleak. I struggled to adapt to the cold weather, which seeped into my body and entered my lungs despite layers of warm clothing. One morning, I awoke to a beautiful day with sunlight shining directly on my face. I got up and looked outside; frost still covered the window and white powder sprinkled the grass. I pulled the panels of the curtains as close together as I could to block the sun and cold and jumped back into bed.

Two days later, I was coughing constantly during the day and having trouble sleeping through the night. The cough soon escalated into bouts of wheezing and shortness of breath, which made it difficult to function. My body ached, and I spent much of my time feeling weak and trying to catch my breath. I also found it harder and harder to move around.

My sister immigrated at the same time and continued through her transition with good health. She walked to and from school every day and didn't have as much trouble adjusting to the cold climate as I did. Although she felt the chill, she did not become ill.

My mother was concerned about me getting sick, and with a furrowed brow she took my temperature. Then, she gave me a range of over-the-counter medications and home remedies to get me through this mysterious illness. I used Vicks Vapor Rub ointment, Canadian Healing Oil, menthol crystals mixed with Vaseline, Musterole ointment, and other familiar remedies used on the island. None of them seemed to work in this new land. We were desperate to find something to get rid of my cough. My mother and I talked about going to a doctor, but we decided against it. A medical visit would have been expensive, and we couldn't afford it. But within a couple of days my condition worsened. I had chills at random times, and the coughing and lack of sleep left me so fatigued I could barely stand up. From time to time, a feeling of sadness came over me. I was upset that I had left my island paradise to be with my family and discover more opportunities, but I had found only cold weather and sickness.

With a worried look on my mother's face, she asked relatives and friends what she could do about the symptoms I was experiencing. One morning, when I woke up, my body ached so bad I didn't have the strength to rise from the bed without assistance. My mother said, "I think you should see a doctor." I was reluctant to go, hoping that I would feel better by the next day, but I was too weak to argue and eventually gave in.

My eldest aunt's friend recommended a doctor in Cambridge, Massachusetts, a few miles away from where we lived in Brighton. She said good things about him and that he was inexpensive — the main reason we went to him, hoping the bill wouldn't drain our meager savings.

I did not have the energy to walk even a few yards or to wait for public transportation, so we took a taxi to the doctor's office — another extravagance. After a thorough examination, the doctor sat across from me in his chair in his office and pronounced, "Young lady, you have nothing more than the common cold." Then he said that maybe the colder climate was making it harder for me to fight off the bacteria.

"Colder weather! We don't have cold weather where I come from," I mumbled to myself. He had good news though; the illness was not serious and easily treatable.

I listened, acknowledging his diagnosis, but I reserved judgment. My illness felt serious, as did the symptoms — an aching body, weakness, breathlessness, wheezing, and coughing. I had trouble accepting that it was a "simple" cold. I didn't believe that his simple solution would work either, but I would not question the man out loud. After all, he was a doctor. He gave me a penicillin injection and two prescriptions and told me that the medicine would restore my good health. If I had known then what I know now, I would not have accepted his word.

After the penicillin injection, and twelve hours after taking the first dose of one of the medications, my face started to get puffy. The swelling spread quickly down my neck and through my body until my ankles were indiscernible from my calves, as if I had been injected with helium. My entire body was bloated. No matter what I ate or drank, I kept nothing down. I was in the bathroom moments later vomiting and having diarrhea at the same time — an experience in itself. I had a strange feeling in my chest that I couldn't explain how it felt and I became very frightened. I was having more trouble breathing than I had before taking the medication.

I hummed Gospel songs and convinced myself that I could pull through if I kept a positive outlook. Despite the reaction, I took the second dose of medication and immediately experienced another problem. I could not urinate no matter how hard I tried. I turned on the water faucet in the bathroom hoping the sound of the running water would help, but I got no relief. I put a few drops of peppermint oil in the toilet bowl hoping to clear my urinary passage, but to no avail. Nothing seemed to help. Between brief spells of sleep, I spent the night trying home remedy after home remedy, frantically searching for a cure for these new ills.

Fatigued and listless when I woke up, I called in sick to my job for the third consecutive day. My absence didn't make my supervisor happy, and I feared that it eroded her confidence in me.

While most people were getting ready for the Christmas Holidays, I spent the day lying in bed, depressed about my health, which seemed not to be improving. I got up only to drink the weak tea my mother had left me before she went to work. She called at intervals throughout the day whenever she got a chance to see if there was any change. During her third call, I told her nothing had changed and I wasn't feeling any better.

Without hesitation she said, "Take a shower and put on some clothes. I'll be home shortly to take you to the hospital." My situation had escalated beyond our control, and the way her voice sounded, I could tell she was worried that my sickness had advanced.

I wasn't about to disagree with my mother. While I got dressed and waited for her, I allowed my worries to overwhelm me. I was terrified thinking about the changes to my body. I had not eaten anything in a full day, and I was weak and still puffy. I didn't believe this was only a "common cold" as the doctor had said, but I hoped the doctors at the hospital would know what to do.

I walked a few yards down the street to the bus stop, leaning on my mother's arm. We had just missed the bus — I saw the back of it driving away. We had to wait about thirty minutes for the next one to arrive. My mother and I boarded the first bus that came by as if we knew where we were going.

She dropped the bus fare into the box, glanced at the driver, and said in a low and urgent tone, "Could you drop us off at the first hospital please?" The driver took one look at my pathetic face and my heaving chest, which must have been enough to convince him that it was serious, and he nodded. When he got close to the nearest hospital, he stopped the bus and instructed us to cross the street and take a left; we would see a hospital to the right. I leaned on my mother's shoulder as we walked into what was known then as the Observation Unit of the New England Deaconess Hospital. I checked in at the front desk and told the receptionist it was an emergency. She asked me for some background information and took notes. Then she told me to sit and a nurse would be with me shortly.

About twenty minutes later, a nurse came to the door and called my name. By then I was gasping for breath worse than when I had left home. I stumbled through the door behind her and my mother followed us. The nurse took my vital signs and asked a few questions about my medical history, and she also asked for the names of medications I had been taking. I handed her the medications prescribed by the other doctor, and then I mentioned that I'd received a penicillin injection at the doctor's office. She made a note of it, left the room, and she was soon replaced by a hospital doctor.

The doctor reviewed the nurse's notes and then examined me. I was in so much pain from not being able to urinate that he catheterized me. He moved quickly and I got the impression there was an urgency to the situation. He looked at me as though he was worried. Then he opened the door and shouted to the nurses' station down the hall. "We need lab tests done on this patient STAT!" No one seemed to be in sight, but I could hear a muttered answer from the other end of the hall, and soon a different nurse hurried into the room.

She told me in quick, short sentences that someone would be with me shortly to draw my blood and run tests on it. The phlebotomist was there in a flash. Her words were rushed, though her actions were slow and steady. I glanced at my mother for support. She shook her head, her eyes large and dark, and I realized she was just as frightened as I by the quick actions of the hospital personnel. Seeing the fear on her face, my heart raced and my breath came in choked sobs. I reached for her hand and she came and stood next to me while my blood was drawn and the nurse left. Every so often, we would hear footsteps outside the door and I looked out, anticipating the doctor or the nurse coming to give us a report of the lab results. But each time, the steps retreated down the hall — I felt like we had been waiting for hours.

The doctor finally returned to the room carrying a folder with a stack of paperwork. "We have the results of the blood tests. You have a kidney infection. It's good you came in when you did!"

He explained this as I sat on the bed twisting my fingers. An allergic reaction to the injection had caused me to stop urinating and had exacerbated a range of symptoms, from the initial cough and breathlessness to the increasing weakness and swelling. It was an "Aha" moment — there really was something wrong.

I swallowed and stared at him. He asked me to follow him to another room and said he would schedule more tests. I was hooked up immediately to an IV and was given glass after glass of cranberry juice, which I'd never had before. I hated the taste and could not pinpoint anything I'd had on the island close to it. The juice was supposedly to help treat the infection and to help flush my kidneys. My veins were small and they wiggled, so I also disliked the process of having the needle pierced into them when the nurse started an IV to transmit medicine through my body.

The whole experience was a nightmare, and I spent most of my time trying not to think about what was happening to me. But I couldn't let go. I asked myself, *Is this my punishment for not questioning the first doctor?*

If I had thought of coming to the hospital sooner, I might have saved myself a great deal of pain and panic. I promised myself that I would act more swiftly in the future and do whatever it took to get over my sickness.

Later that day, my wristband was replaced with a different room and floor number. I was admitted officially for further observation and a battery of tests. I wondered whether the IV and cranberry juice had worked. I started to feel better; it was getting easier to breathe even though the swelling had not gone down completely. I lost the panicky feeling of not knowing what was going on and felt more secure. A few minutes after I was in my new room, a phlebotomist came and took more blood samples. I watched nervously, musing that I was becoming a pincushion, and wondering how much blood I would have left by the end of her ministrations.

The new test results showed that my kidneys were not functioning as they should be. I was spilling protein in my urine, which indicated that a problem was occurring somewhere in my blood or urinary system. The doctor said it was one of the earliest signs of kidney damage. I was astonished; it came as a shock to me, and I stared at the doctor. I could not remember being bedridden in my entire life. When I had a cold, I always recovered quickly. My mother and grandmother treated me themselves, and I was never too sick to stay home from school.

I had no familiarity with the medical profession or understanding of their terminology. I had no idea what "spilling protein" meant or how serious it was. When I asked the doctor, he hesitated for a moment and said something was going on with my kidneys. He may have observed that I was scared and did not want an explanation to frighten me any further.

Soon after he left the room, a nurse entered and told me I would be scheduled for a kidney biopsy. When I asked what that was, she explained, "It is a procedure to take a small piece of your kidney for further testing." This terrified me even more and I spent a restless, sleepless night.

The next morning, the doctor came to my room to inform me that instead of a needle biopsy to take tissue and fluid samples from the kidney, which could be done in the room, I would go to the OR to have it done. Within an hour, I was taken in and prepped as if I were having major surgery. I would receive general anesthesia — another new concept for me.

After the biopsy, I woke up sobbing. The nurse in the recovery room assured me it was normal and handed me a tissue. "Lots of people wake up crying, dear. I'll go and get the doctor and let him know you're awake." The biopsy left a long horizontal scar on the left side of my back.

When the doctor came, he told me the surgery had gone well, that there had been no complications, and they had already run some tests on my kidney.

"You have glomerulonephritis *(glo-mer-u-lo-nuh-FRI-tis)*." He said the word slowly, but with no explanation about how the laboratory analysis would impact my life. The word — the idea itself — confused me, an island girl. Living in the middle of a metropolis didn't mean I would understand large medical words and this word — a whopping seven syllables — sounded bad. When I returned to my room, I asked a nurse if she had a medical dictionary she could lend me. I thumbed through it desperately searching for the word I thought I'd heard and eventually found it.

Glomerulonephritis is a syndrome in which the kidneys are inflamed and lose their ability to remove waste and excess fluid from the body. I learned that I was allergic to penicillin, which had caused the reaction in my body. I was baffled and I could not help wondering how an injection led to a system-wide problem in my body, causing a decrease in my kidney function, building more toxins in my blood, and poisoning my body. If I had waited any longer to come to the hospital, I would have died. As time went on, I found out I have many allergies — name it, and I'm allergic to it.

During the two weeks I spent in the hospital, I thought my kidneys were improving. At least I was urinating on my own, but my kidneys weren't performing their normal functions. In the meantime, I had two "cut-down" procedures — a small cut to a vein to insert a tube for drawing blood and receiving medication. The doctor said there was no way around this, and he was doing it to make the process quicker and easier. It meant that I wouldn't have to endure constant sticks. One incision was to the right side of my neck and required five to seven stitches to close. The second incision was in my left arm and also needed five to seven stitches. The procedures were painful and equally uncomfortable. I cried each time the doctor did the procedure, and I hated having to look at those cuts.

I thought the nurses were either very kind or very absentminded. This made my stay sometimes pleasant and then sometimes tortuous. A day after the biopsy, a nurse attempting to flush my urinary catheter accidentally injected Benzalkonium Solution, an antiseptic, instead of water. It burned as though a fire was running through me. When I screamed, she asked me what was the matter and I told her the solution was burning badly. She looked at the label on the container. A look of utter shock drained the color from her face. She apologized, told me it was the wrong solution, and said she would be right back.

She returned with a more experienced nurse who also apologized. The experienced nurse inserted another solution into the attached IV and flushed out the remnants of the wrong solution. Then she flushed the catheter and told me the new solution would stop the burning. About an hour later the pain subsided, which was a huge relief. A doctor visited me later in the day and also apologized for his nurse's mishap. The next day, a female nurse's aide who usually visited me in the morning before she started her shift came by to ask how I was feeling. She said the staff had heard about what had happened to me the day before, and the supervisor warned them to be more careful. I thought I would see the nurse who made the mistake, but I did not see her for a few days. I suspected she may have been disciplined so I inquired about her. A nurse told me she was off duty for a few days and would be in training when she returned.

One morning, to my surprise, the nurse's aide brought me a mini transistor radio, as small as a baby's hand, and earphones. She said she was thinking of me on her way home from work, and she wanted to get something that might help to cheer me up. I listened to the radio for the rest of my time there, finding comfort and escape in the music.

Chapter 2

Moving Forward

$\mathcal{I}$ received my discharge at the end of two weeks, an outpatient appointment, and a prescription for Prednisone, an anti-inflammatory steroid. Still frightened about my health issues, I did not return to work. I wasn't sure I was ready to enter the outside world. In these early stages of my kidney problem and the medical challenges before me, I sat at home for days on end, staring at the four walls of my room, while my mind wandered with vivid recollections of the home I had left behind. I would lie on the sofa in a fetal position for comfort and take quick naps, which helped keep me from thinking constantly about my illness.

One day, during my second week at home, something came over me and I felt the urge to return to work as soon as possible to get my life back on track. I told myself that if I took the new medication and kept my appointments with the doctor, I would be fine. I knew enough by then to realize I would spend at least part of my life fighting this illness. I needed to be prepared mentally and financially, and a good job was the best place to start. I looked for a new job with health insurance benefits and a higher salary than my previous job to help defray my medical bills.

It was now March 1970, and I woke up to the blue sky, the green grass poking through the snow, and the trees beginning to bloom. I saw these things as signs for a new beginning and re-engaging into the world with a hopeful heart. My confidence was well founded. I acquired a new job almost immediately with a telecommunications company and started the following week. I was relieved that I did not have to reveal my health challenge to the employer for fear I would be considered a risk.

A week after I went to work, which was a month after my discharge, I received the hospital bill. Attached to it was a claim notice from the insurance company stating that my insurance was not effective until two days after my admission and that I was ineligible for coverage. Therefore, I was responsible for the bill reaching upward of $17,000!

In disbelief, I gasped, "Oh no!" I contacted the hospital to double-check if there might have been an error in billing. The supervisor informed me that the charges were correct, so I made arrangements to make monthly payments. None of the charges were forgiven; this was a financial hardship that took me several years to pay off.

Many friends and relatives tried to convince my mother and me to file a negligence lawsuit against the doctor who gave me the penicillin injection and put my life at risk so he could be held responsible for paying the hospital bill, but we decided against that course of action even though he caused me a world of frustration and pain. Suing was unheard of in my native country then, and it wasn't our desire to seek money from a doctor for his unintentional deed. I was concerned about getting healthy and moving on with my life, not summoning him into court and assigning blame.

One summer evening, while I was at home watching television, my mouth started to feel extremely dry. I took a two-liter bottle of soda water from the refrigerator, sat on the sofa, and drank the entire bottle. Then I felt overstuffed and uncomfortable. It was difficult for me to get up to get ready for bed, so I slept on the sofa and dragged myself across the floor to the bathroom when nature called.

After that, a few times I felt nauseous on my way to work and returned home each time, as well as getting ill at work and being sent home. On more than one occasion, I collapsed on the job and was transported by ambulance to the hospital. Up to this time, my supervisor still didn't know the nature of my illness, but she was aware that I had some health issues. I did not tell my friends at the company of my medical condition for fear that my sickness would get back to the supervisor. I had a whole range of pressures: trying not to get suspended or fired for poor attendance, getting to work on time to avoid being suspended, and worrying about my medical condition. I worried constantly, and my worrying brought with it another group of physical symptoms.

Worrying caused my fears to build up, and the anxiety caused severe stomach cramps. At times they were so bad that I thought I might be dying. I was hospitalized on a few occasions for a nervous stomach. At one of my hospital admissions, the doctor asked what was bothering me, but before I could answer, he said abruptly, "You have to get over your fears. I can see it all over your face, and your worrying is going to cause more health problems. Stop worrying. We will take care of you. There's nothing for you to worry about — let us do the worrying. It's our job." His mouthful of words took me by surprise and gave me a feeling of relief that he was concerned with my well-being.

I mentioned his comments to a co-worker, one of my closest friends. The following day, she brought me a "Thinking of You" card with a handwritten message and poem inside. The poem, "Why Worry" reads:

There are only two things to worry about…

Either you are well or you are sick

If you are well—then there is
  nothing to worry about

If you are sick—then there are
  two things to worry about…

Either you will get better or you will die

If you get better—then there is
  nothing to worry about

If you die—then there are
  two things to worry about…

You will either go to heaven or go to hell

If you go to heaven—then there is
  nothing to worry about...

If you go to hell—you'll be so damn busy
  shaking hands

You won't have time to worry—
  so why worry?

— *Author unknown*

At the end of the poem, she drew a row of smiley faces. I chuckled yet felt sad at the same time. The words were fitting — I would get better or I wouldn't; I would get fired or remain on the job. No amount of worrying would change either of those situations. I took home the poem and pinned it to my bedroom wall. It touched me so much that I kept it through the years.

Through all these ups and downs, I was still uninformed about my disease. I convinced myself that the doctor at the hospital was wrong in his diagnosis so I sought a second opinion. I told the new doctor I wanted to know if I had kidney disease or if something else was causing my physical distress. He listened to my concerns, and then he telephoned the previous doctor and requested copies of my file to be faxed to him.

Meanwhile, he ordered new lab tests. The new tests confirmed the previous doctor's diagnosis; I did have a kidney problem, and there were no other signs of illness. After he explained what the results meant, I perceived that my kidneys were about to shut down any minute and that I was in serious danger. I had more confidence in this new doctor and vowed to see him from then on. I visited him every three months. The nurse took my vital signs, and the doctor ordered blood and urine tests. Occasionally he wrote new prescriptions that I thought were counteracting the problem.

Over time, I noticed that the prescribed amounts were increasing in dosage and asked him about it. His vague answers led me to believe that he was hiding something from me or that he was telling me some truth but not all of it. I quickly lost trust in him and went to a third doctor.

Thus began a cycle of doctor hunting — finding a new doctor and quickly losing faith in previous ones. This made it hard for me to be content with my treatment and even harder to trust the medical profession.

At the beginning of 1974, within several weeks of changing doctors, my newest doctor ordered blood tests, which were taken and analyzed the same day at his location. He seemed concerned with the results and wanted to discuss them with his colleagues. The next day he called and said he was admitting me to the hospital with which he was affiliated, because it was better equipped to handle my situation than his small practice. I did not expect to hear this type of news, but I accepted his decision.

After spending a few days in the hospital, there was no change in my health or prognosis. When he came by, he suggested trying "something new." There was one caveat to this something new — it may or may not help my condition, and it may be a placebo — a fake pill. Then he said, "It may grow hair on your face and possibly your body."

I was incoherent at the time, after being awakened, and I wasn't sure whether to take him seriously. But the description horrified me. I was afraid to take the risk and did not sign the release form to allow the new pill. It was more than I could stand, and when he left the room abruptly without uttering another word, I burst into tears. When my mother came to visit me, she noticed that I had been crying and asked what was wrong. Sulking, I replied, "The doctor wants me to sign a form to try a new medication, but I did not sign it because I may end up looking like a monkey. He left without saying anything."

By this time I was swollen with fluid retention. The doctor had left without writing the order to have my fluids withdrawn. I was feeling miserable; my skin was stinging and itching. It was my body's normal reaction to fluid buildup, but I never got used to the unpleasant feeling. My mother was not pleased, so she pressed the call button and asked the nurse to page the doctor for treatment. The nurse paged the doctor several times, but he did not respond. At 8:00 P.M., when visiting hours were over, my mother told me to get dressed; she was taking me home.

It was late when I reached home, and I was eager to go to bed after the stressful day, but I craved fresh coconut water, although I was already full of fluid. Even though I was cautious of my fluid intake, I drank a small glass of the coconut water and went to bed. I was hoping that during the night I would urinate sufficiently to decrease my bladder, but I released only a few drops, and sleep was incredibly difficult. The thick, full feeling made it feel like I would explode. No matter which side I laid on, the fluid accumulated on that side of my face making it very puffy and awful looking. When morning came, I was in quite a bit of pain so I stayed inside the house, hoping for a miracle.

The swelling ran through my entire body, causing my stomach and back to protrude. My skin was so sensitive it hurt no matter where something touched me. I was perplexed and hoping the swelling would dissipate eventually, but it did not. When my mother came home from work and saw my condition, she immediately called a taxicab to take me to the hospital where I had first been diagnosed with the kidney problem. I was ashamed to go back to that hospital. I was afraid that the doctors and other medical staff might recognize my name from the previous hospitalizations, and I was also embarrassed by my appearance.

Nurses watched me struggling to get onto the stretcher and insisted on helping me. It took four of them to transfer me from the stretcher to a bed, each of them holding one of the four corners of the sheets. They moved me back and forth for examination and to perform certain tests, and they did their best to make me comfortable. Later on, I was admitted to a room, and a nurse inserted a catheter so the small amount of urine I was putting out could drain freely from my bladder.

The next morning, I awoke to find that I was breathless. A nurse put in a request to the doctor to remove the fluid from my lungs. For the procedure, a nurse wheeled in a cart with covered items while I sat on the left side of the bed with an adjustable bed table in front of me. She placed a pillow on top of the table to put my arms around and told me to buckle myself in a fetal position. As I positioned my upper body over the table, I held my breath and wondered how much it would hurt. I got a glimpse of a long needle on the cart and asked what it was for.

"That's how we're going to get the fluid out of your lungs, honey," the nurse said without hesitation. She pointed to a plastic container on the cart. "We'll put it in there to send to the lab."

I held my head down, wishing I hadn't asked or seen the needle. The doctor told me to get ready, and I felt the small pinch of the anesthetic needle. It numbed my back so I wouldn't feel the pain of the larger needle being used to remove the fluid. He then inserted the larger needle into my back and warned me I could not move during the procedure. If I did, I could become paralyzed. I held extremely still, gripping my pillow. Thoughts flooded in and subsided like waves. Ten minutes later, it was over. It had been an uncomfortable feeling, but it wasn't as painful as I had expected. Best of all, I could breathe normally again. I lay back on the bed with a sigh of relief, feeling somewhat normal.

In the evening, the nephrologist who treated me during my initial visit to the hospital came by. He asked, "Where have you been?" I did not want him to know I was like a "Doubting Thomas" and had sought out other doctors to get second and even third opinions. I was afraid that if I let him know about my hunt, he wouldn't give me his full attention. I said I had returned to my country, which I had, but it was not for an extended period of time as may have come across. He seemed to accept my excuse, and it put me at ease.

He removed my chart from the bedside, reviewed it, and laid the story out frankly. My kidneys were failing slowly but surely, and they were far more deteriorated than they had been the last time he saw me. They were withering like a prune. Looking over his glasses, he said, "When that happens, you'll have to live on a special machine to clean the toxins and waste from your blood."

After careful consideration and thought about what he said, I felt as if he knew the intimate details of what was going on with my illness, and suddenly I trusted his judgment. I remembered at one of my prior visits, he had mentioned that my kidneys would eventually shut down in about five years. My kidneys were at their end — there was severely reduced functionality and I was facing chronic renal failure. I felt that my symptoms confirmed his diagnosis. I had trouble keeping my eyes open for long periods of time, and I found myself nodding off frequently no matter where I was. I was of the opinion that this was caused by the toxins in my blood putting me to sleep when they got to my brain.

While I was still hospitalized, the doctor prescribed a new diuretic medication after I had taken several others that didn't seem to work anymore. The new one was the most effective, but it came at a price; the new medication had dire side effects, and receiving the injections caused me a lot of stress — an excruciating urinating pain. I had no other choice than to suffer the consequences of taking it. It was administered via a Heparin Lock, a tube attached to a catheter inserted into my wrist, which helped to keep the blood flowing and helped to prevent blood clots in the catheter. It was not a relaxing wait while I remained in the hospital waiting for the doctor to research a possible choice of treatment for my release.

Meanwhile, a friend sent me a jar of dried fruits, which consisted of raisins, apricots, bananas, peaches, etc. — something I had not eaten for quite a while. I was so elated to receive them that I ate several pieces right away. It proved to be a big mistake. When my doctor received my lab results, my potassium level had skyrocketed. He rushed to my room with a look of concern and wanted to know what I had eaten or drank. He observed the dried fruit jar on the table and picked it up. He read the contents and then put down the jar and said, "No more of the candy for the time being; your potassium has escalated and is very high. It could have been the potato and other foods you ate yesterday, and the dried fruits. It's not good for you. I'll have the dietitian come and see you."

I was disappointed, but despite my feelings, I understood. I was not in the best of health, and I didn't want to make things worse. But, I had been craving variety in my boring diet of hospital food and had planned to eat the dried fruits as an alternative. As soon as he left the room, my mother put the jar in her bag to take home. I looked at her with a frown, sighed, and shook my head as if to say I couldn't believe she was taking it away.

She smiled, "It's for your own good."

Within several minutes of the doctor leaving, the renal dietitian came to my room. She put me on a strict diet. She was so insistent that I can still remember her saying, "Only three ounces of meat or fish; no more than five nuts a day, no salt, a small serving of vegetables or fruits, and a limited amount of dairy products."

I listened to her advice and made a promise to be more careful with my intake. I consoled myself that I would soon be well enough to eat what I wanted — whenever I wanted.

Even though I did not have a big appetite, and although I had promised to watch what I ate and drank, I still yearned for certain foods that were off limits, and they were almost impossible to ignore. My body was having a hard enough time already, so I justified filling the void by telling myself that if I was craving something, it was probably a sign that my body needed it. The small amount of food I was getting was not enough to keep me full until the next meal.

I called my sister one afternoon around the time she arrived home from school to tell her I was hungry. The food served wasn't tasty and the diet was challenging. I asked her to bring me something to eat. She did not live far from the hospital, and within minutes she and one of my cousins who lived next door brought me onion rings and a Whopper from Burger King. We planned carefully so I wouldn't get caught with the prohibited meal. My cousin stood by the door, keeping a sharp lookout for nurses and doctors, and my sister sat on the bed on the side closest to the door, blocking me with her body in case anyone came through.

We believed that we had covered all the bases, and I sank my teeth into the hamburger. It was the best meal away from home I had tasted in a while, and I still rank it as one of my finest snacks. The flavor was one hundred times better than any food in the hospital. The condiments on the burger made my saliva flow since I wasn't allowed to have them. I tore through the burger like wind through the trees, eating as quickly as I could with one eye on my cousin at the door. Although we had covered the room physically, we were not thinking that the smell would travel down the hall to the nurses' station. It must have made its way there slowly as I was almost finished when a nurse came into the room. She did not pass directly in front of me; she walked toward the other patient in the semi-private room.

"I smell something good," she said looking around. None of us spoke or glanced at one another. By the time she came over to me and asked how lunch was, I had already given the remainder of the burger to my sister. She was taking the final bite and about to crumple the paper, making the nurse believe she'd been the one eating in the room. I was glad when the nurse left and didn't ask to take my temperature, since she would have smelled the onions on my breath. I came close to getting caught, and I wasn't willing to go through the embarrassment of another lecture on food, so it was the first and last time I asked my sister to smuggle food to me.

The other patient in the room had hot flashes and frequently opened the window next to her. It was winter, which caused the room to become beastly cold. As soon as nurses came through the door, they turned around and returned wearing sweaters. When the window was closed, the wind blew through the cracks in the window frame and made me shiver. When it became unbearable, I told one of them that I was cold, so she got some blankets and plugged up the windows.

When the doctor discharged me the next day, a day earlier than I expected, I was overjoyed. By this time, I had received only two new treatments and certainly was not healed, but I was ready to go home and get back into my routine. I got up early, took a shower, and got ready, thinking I was leaving the hospital soon after breakfast. After sitting on the bed for about twenty minutes, the nurse came to tell me the doctor would be with me shortly. I waited and waited, very anxious to leave, and wondered what the doctor could possibly have to say. He had already given me a list, through the dietitian, of the foods I should avoid, how much fluid to drink, including the all-important cranberry juice. He hadn't done any major procedures, so certainly there could be no instructions about taking care of wounds or surgical sites. I was left alone for most of the morning to wonder if there was something new. When he came, he said he wanted me to have a blood transfusion before I left. My prior lab results showed that I was anemic — an iron deficiency that made me tired most of the time and could worsen the problems I already had to handle. The obvious choice, in his opinion, was to have the blood transfusion to strengthen my blood.

I thought about his recommendation for several minutes. I was sure that having a transfusion would mean I had to spend more time in the hospital and I was ready to go home. *If I am iron deficient*, I reasoned, *the most natural remedy is to eat foods high in iron, and take an iron supplement*. I had made up my mind, and no amount of doctoring was going to make me change it. I shook my head and said, "No, I decline; I'll eat the right foods at home to build up my blood." He tried to persuade me that the transfusion would work faster, but I refused to accept it.

It was close to noon when I received my discharge papers. On my way home, the wheels were spinning in my stubborn head; self-doubt struck, and I wondered if I should have accepted the transfusion. Did I make a mistake that I would come to regret, a situation where I would end up in the hospital again by being headstrong and not accepting the transfusion? I calmed myself down with the belief that I would still be in the hospital accepting someone's blood if I had taken the transfusion, and I wouldn't be on my way home. The most important thing to me at this juncture was to live my life as best I could, regardless of my illness. At this point, I wanted to live in the outside world and didn't want to spend any more of my days cooped up.

I convinced myself that I had done the right thing, and I got off the bus before my regular stop to go to the grocery store. I bought items on the list that the dietitian had recommended and other foods that are high in iron. I also bought Guinness Stout. I remembered hearing that it was rich in iron. I didn't know if it was true or if it was simply fiction, however, I wanted to try practically anything.

I knew that my aunt in Barbados would seek effective local products that build blood. As soon as I reached home, I called her with my request. She sent me a Tonic Wine with added iron, as well as a Beef, Iron & Wine Supplement that was popular on the island. I spent the next month eating iron-heavy foods and matching each meal with the wines.

When I returned for my follow-up visit, the doctor reviewed my lab results and sat up straight in his chair with a surprised look. It made me think he was puzzled by the results, which showed that my hemoglobin — the blood iron levels — had improved. I was no longer anemic, but my numbers were still below the normal range. It didn't seem as though he thought I could have done this naturally, and he was surprised that my numbers had boosted in such a short span of time without the blood transfusion. Determined to reach the normal range quickly, I continued to drink Guinness, drink the wines, and eat the iron-building foods.

On my next visit, six months after my discharge, my hemoglobin results were finally in the normal range. The doctor glanced at my lab results and said, "Your iron has gone way up. What have you been taking?"

I grinned at him and replied, "Foods such as spinach, beets, wine my aunt sent me, and I drink Stout."

He shook his head and chuckled, "You Caribbean people have a remedy for everything."

Medicine has its place and can do amazing things, but some medical specialists don't always like it when holistic and homeopathic remedies are used. I did appreciate his sense of humor about it though.

The look on his face indicated he was pleased with my progress, and it seemed as though he supported what I was doing, although he did not say it. He didn't seem to fully understand why I had become anemic, but he told me to be careful with my diet regarding my iron intake and to maintain my current schedule of eating. His words made me feel more comfortable with him as my nephrologist. He became the one I turned to first when I had questions and concerns related to my health.

As time went on, I grew more and more worried about my physical well-being and wondered if I would ever recover completely. My eyesight was failing and I went through many days with blurred vision. I thought I was going blind, and it reminded me of my father's occasional blindness before his death. I had to be helped while boarding public transportation; my legs felt too weak to propel me up the steps on my own, which took an emotional toll on me. My sister left home for school the same time I went to work, so she could help me onto the bus or streetcar.

There was a time when I lost the ability to sleep or lie in bed for long periods. Every now and then my body would get puffy with fluid, and that feeling kept me from stretching out or lying down comfortably. I would sleep sitting on the floor in a corner of the bedroom, where I could position myself against the walls for better comfort. But no matter how I sat or placed myself, I was uncomfortable and fidgety after a short time, which added more stress to an already upsetting situation. The stress from the pain and discomfort, compounded with the exhaustion of too little sleep and the worry over my eyesight, pulled my health and mental strength downward.

One night, after I tossed and turned on the floor for several hours and had become too restless to stay still, I tried to sleep in my bed again. Before I lay down, my mother, who believes in miracles, opened some of the evangelist Oral Roberts' magazines to specific pages with messages of faith, hope, and healing. She spread them under the sheet so I would lie on them. I lay down and turned over a few times; then, suddenly, I felt as though a heavy weight had been lifted off my body. I sighed in great relief, feeling relaxed for the first time in months. From that night on I slept in my bed. I don't know whether it was mental, physical, emotional, or if it was a miracle, but it was my belief that the magazines comforted me and eased the pain of the swelling from my body. Once I was able to get enough sleep, I began to feel better and to believe in the possibility of healing. I went into each day with renewed vigor and a greater passion, hoping a cure would be found for my illness.

Chapter 3

Confronting Dialysis

To my amazement, Thanksgiving Day in the USA was similar to the Christmas Day feast in my native country of Barbados. On that day in 1974, I felt healthy enough to help with some of the food preparation and take part in the festivities, which I hadn't been able to enjoy the previous year. I always had a small appetite, but on that day I acted like a glutton yet conscientious in my selections. I felt determined to enjoy every second of the holiday with my health going through serious changes, and I didn't know how much longer I had to live.

The next year, Thanksgiving marked a critical point in my illness and became an important milestone in my life. The progression of my ill health had reached its worst point and my visits to the doctor increased in frequency — from every two months to once a month. A week before Thanksgiving Day, I went to the clinic to have routine lab work done — another necessary chore in my life. The results indicated stage five of my illness — severely reduced kidney function. However, nothing else in my body besides this had reared its ugly head. I didn't have any additional symptoms that indicated I had reached another stage: 5.

The day after the tests, I received a call at work from my nephrologist's nurse. She told me that I would be admitted to the hospital the next day and that she'd get back to me with the time of admission. Startled, I asked to speak to my doctor. I had questions for him that I didn't think the nurse would answer. I wanted to know what was going on with my health, what had triggered the urgent need for my admission to the hospital, and if it could wait until after Thanksgiving, only one week away.

When the doctor picked up the phone, he told me my blood chemistry was bad; my kidneys weren't filtering the toxins out, and it would negatively affect me soon. He needed to get me into the hospital to start on dialysis as soon as possible.

I was puzzled, and in a nervous and worried tone, I shouted, "Dialysis! What is that?"

His voice became gentler as he apparently realized how frightening this must be for me, "You'll be hooked up to a machine to clean your blood. The machine will get rid of the toxins and you'll feel much better."

I nodded as if he could see me. The thought of being connected to a machine seemed horrifying and painful. I was shaking, and my eyes filled with tears. Still perplexed and perturbed, I asked him what had changed so drastically that I needed to go through this procedure all of a sudden and does it happen to all kidney patients. I had hoped to avoid living on a machine.

"We'll talk about it when I see you at the hospital. Don't worry; everything will be fine."

I detected sympathy in his voice, but he hung up the phone before I could ask another question. I put the phone down and paused for a moment. I didn't think I should keep the news to myself; I needed to get it off my shoulders. I called my mother at work to tell her, instead of waiting until I reached home.

"Take it easy," she told me. "Don't worry; we'll see this through together. We'll talk about it when I get home."

I then walked over to my supervisor's desk to let her know that my doctor had scheduled me for admission to the hospital the next day. She seemed concerned. She put down her cup, and asked me if I knew how long.

I shrugged, "I don't know."

Her response was, "Keep me posted."

After work, I went directly home and gathered some necessities for another admission to the hospital, this time to undergo what I envisioned as my most serious procedure so far.

I was admitted to the Palmer 2 building of the New England Deaconess Hospital. While I was in the room unpacking my belongings, the urologist entered and introduced himself. He had been referred by my nephrologist to do the procedure in preparation for dialysis, but he needed to examine me first. After a brief examination, he found that my veins were too small and wouldn't offer the stable foundation that is required for dialysis, so he decided to implant a fistula (Diagram A) in my left arm. The fistula is also called a bovine graft — a cow's artery used as a connection between an artery and a vein. Initially, he seemed a little reluctant to explain, but he said the fistula provides a dependable access point for the dialysis needle, which is placed under the skin of the arm for the most convenient positioning.

Fistula (A)

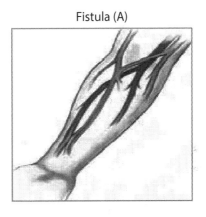

I listened nervously with my head bent over looking at the floor. I didn't like the idea of a cow's artery in my body, and I didn't like the thought of dialysis either. I tried not to think about it too much. The whirlwind of activity around me was excessive and the options too upsetting. It was better, I thought, to turn my brain off and go with the flow, meaning the least upsetting for me and possibly the best recovery. When he finished explaining how the process worked, I reached for the water pitcher, poured a cup full, and took a few gulps. He asked if I had questions.

I said, "No."

He shook my hand and left the room.

In the evening the nurse came to the room and said, "You'll be going to surgery early in the morning. Take your shower before you retire for the night."

After I showered, the nurse's aide brought me a few Graham crackers and a glass of milk, and later she returned to give me a back rub. When I got up to use the bathroom, which I thought was in the middle of the night, I returned to find the orderly in the room waiting to wheel me away to the OR to get the fistula inserted into my arm. It was nothing like I imagined it would be. The anesthesia didn't work. I could raise my arm, so the anesthesiologist injected more of the numbing solution into the IV. When the procedure started, I was fully awake and my arm still wasn't completely numb. Maybe I was supposed to be in twilight instead of fully numb. I felt the pressure when the surgeon made the first incision close to my wrist and the second incision close to the front of my elbow.

I lay there crying silently for almost the entire procedure, which took approximately four hours. When the surgeon was almost done, he realized that the fistula didn't work and he reopened one of the incisions. By that time, I had been lying there about three hours feeling the pressure and hearing everything going on around me. It was tedious and nerve-racking, and I didn't want to take it any longer, but I had no choice other than to endure it. Adding to my discomfort, the surgeon was unhappy with me crying and told me it wasn't helping him. Luckily for me the fistula worked the second time, and I was out of surgery about an hour later.

An OR nurse took me back to my room where I focused on calming myself down, but my arm hurt terribly, making it difficult for me to relax. A nurse on the floor came to my room and said, "I know you're in pain, but we can't give you any painkillers since you're allergic to them."

I responded in a melancholy tone, "Maybe it would have been better if he had cut off my arm." I tried to sleep, knowing that if I were asleep I wouldn't feel the pain or worry about my arm.

The surgeon came by later. When he touched the fistula, which was showing clearly through my skin, and placed his stethoscope on it, he observed that it was moving up and down like a rapid heartbeat. It vibrated constantly as though it had a mind of its own. It startled me, but he gave me a thumbs-up and echoed a medical term, "Your bruit (pronounced *broo-ee)* sounds great." When he realized I would not understand the lingo, he quickly said, "It's working great; you're all set."

I watched it for a while after he left, hypnotized by the rhythmic beating of my heart and the blood passing through the fistula. When curious people touched the fistula and felt the strong vibration, they would quickly step back. The staff could no longer use that arm for blood pressure reading, venipuncture, or IV use, and the head nurse on the floor placed a warning above my bed for the hospital staff.

The first day after the fistula was implanted, I asked the nurse to bandage my arm so I could take a shower. She suggested taking a bath instead to decrease the chance of soapy water leaking through the cover over the incision. She explained that to avoid infection, the incisions shouldn't be exposed to any outside materials. Within twenty-four hours, it was obvious I hadn't been careful enough, because the incision close to the elbow became infected.

That morning, I was scheduled for emergency peritoneal dialysis and transferred from my room to the Intensive Care Unit (ICU) to receive the treatment. I was apprehensive and my fears outweighed my curiosity. My body was full of toxins and my nephrologist seemed eager to start treatment, but before the treatment began, a minor operation was required to make a way into my belly area. He was kind and thoughtful, and he asked me if I wanted him to operate or if I would prefer the doctor from my native country that was doing his internship there. I chose my nephrologist. He had more experience and I was familiar with him. He numbed the area and made a small incision below my belly button. Then he inserted a tube into the lower part of my abdomen to carry the dialysis cleaning solution back and forth. This was another unpleasant experience, despite the numbing medication. I felt as though the tube was piercing my insides. I was immediately ready for dialysis and hooked up to the tube via the intravenous setup, with a plastic bag containing the cleaning solution.

It was pumped into my blood to absorb the toxins, waste products, and extra fluid, and then flushed out (see Diagram B, page 60). The process was repeated several times to fully cleanse my blood while being monitored at the nurses' station.

Everything seemed to be going according to plan, and then something went wrong. The staff forgot to check the equipment periodically to make sure it was functioning as it should. Unexpectedly, I lost energy and felt lethargic and weak, but I thought it was part of the process. My mother stopped by earlier than usual and found me helpless. I recall telling her I felt tired and my body ached. It felt as if a truck had crushed it. I couldn't move my body freely and my fingers and toes were clenched tightly. She marched to the nurses' station to request that someone check on me.

When the nurse read my chart and looked at the equipment, her countenance changed. She dashed through the door and returned a moment later with plastic bags of liquid which she attached to the IV. When my mother asked her what happened and why, she replied that the machine was operating at a higher rate than necessary. It had removed too much fluid from my body too quickly, causing my body to go into a state of shock. She told me that the liquid she added would correct the mistake and bring my body back to its natural state. I began to feel better and within an hour or so, I could wiggle my fingers and toes and the pain had ceased. The next morning, I returned to my room.

Due to the blunder, I missed ordering dinner, and, to my surprise, a nurse went to the public cafeteria and brought me a turkey club sandwich. "This is on the house," she told me.

It was much tastier than the one on the patients' menu. Although I felt so much better at completion of the treatment, as my doctor had assured me, the incident didn't sit well with me — another nurse flaw. How many more nurse mishaps would I have to tolerate before my body returned to normalcy? This ordeal certainly didn't give me any consolation about what was coming next — hemodialysis treatments.

On Thanksgiving Day around 6:00 A.M., a nurse woke me up to get ready for my first hemodialysis treatment, scheduled at 7:00 A.M. I was the only patient in the dialysis unit, with one nurse on duty. She explained how the machines worked, but I was too scared to pay attention to her speech. "The machines look like washing machines," I told her.

She laughed, "That's a good comparison; they are called dialyzers, also known as the artificial kidney."

Although I was petrified in this large room surrounded by machines, she joked with me and made me laugh while she connected the fistula in my arm to one of them (see Diagram C). My blood flowed through the filter inside the machine to remove the waste products and then returned the cleansed blood to my body through the dialyzer. It's the same function as peritoneal dialysis but with a slightly different delivery.

Peritoneal Dialysis (B)

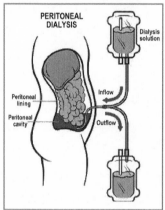

Hemodialysis (C)

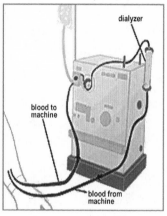

Not knowing what to expect, despite her explanation, it was traumatic — just laying there in a room, surrounded by all that equipment, and having a machine clean your blood. I kept my head under the white sheet and took naps through most of the treatment, which lasted four hours. I didn't feel any pain or any sensation of my blood going back and forth. At the end of the treatment, the nurse announced I would be dialyzed twice a week: Mondays and Thursdays. I returned to my room feeling better except for a headache.

I had to spend Thanksgiving Day in the hospital, so I asked my mother to bring me some of the leftovers and to invite relatives to come with her. A cousin and one of my aunts arrived with her around 4:30 P.M. My mother brought a container full of food, but before I could eat it, the head nurse on the floor called the renal dietitian to make sure it was within my diet restrictions. I thought I was capable of judging what was and wasn't safe for me to eat or drink, but the nurse wanted a professional opinion.

I hadn't eaten the hospital food at lunchtime and I was hungry. I grumbled that the dietitian was taking too long. When she came, she approved everything as I had expected, and I made a joke with her about me knowing the right foods to eat. My mother had brought food that matched my diet requirements, and she was conscientious in her portions. Instead of the American traditional

Thanksgiving dinner, I had my favorite meat — baked pork in place of turkey, stuffing made from crackers, dry pigeon peas in rice instead of mashed potatoes, and French green beans. She didn't bring me a dessert, knowing I was confined to a specific amount of sweets daily.

When I finished eating, I counted the years and the steady progression of my illness in Thanksgiving holidays. It was the time of year when I became sickest and sought the most medical attention, but also the time of year when our family got together and showed appreciation for one another. This had already taken on an importance in my life.

Toward the end of my medical care in the hospital, I had a surprising moment. One evening, my room was flooded with staff members: doctors, nurses, and even technicians. They marched into my room as a group, singing "Happy Birthday", followed by the head nurse carrying a chocolate cake, a knife, a cake server, and small plates on a tray. She put the cake on the adjustable table, placed it in front of me with three candles, and said, "Make a wish and blow out the candles." Then she handed me the knife to cut the cake. She allowed me to take only a sliver of it while the guests took large slices. It was a measure of my time there and the thoughtfulness of the staff that they would acknowledge my birthday and go out of their way to celebrate with me.

One of the doctors joked, "Next year you'll have a new kidney, and you'll be celebrating with your family and friends."

I smiled and said, "I'll hold you to it."

In the back of my mind, I was wishing and hoping it would be a reality.

I returned to work the week after my discharge and informed my supervisor that I would be absent two days a week for dialysis treatment. But I offered to work longer hours during the other days to make up for any backlog, and she welcomed my solution. I was now a dialysis outpatient at the hospital, and my treatments, scheduled from 7:00 A.M. to 11:00 A.M., became a weekly part of my life. I had mentioned to the dialysis staff that I couldn't sleep on the night prior to my treatment, and I couldn't wait for morning to come to get it over with, so I would have either three or four day intervals between treatments to loosen up. I did not take the treatments well; they were distinctly unpleasant, and it was always a struggle for me to accept them. Sometimes they left me feeling tired and sometimes with a headache. I never got accustomed to the idea of my blood needing to be cleansed and having to depend on a mechanical device to stay alive.

It was difficult to get over feeling sorry for myself. I seldom smiled and was so dispirited that I refused to talk with other patients and the staff. Interestingly, the patients that dialyzed at the same time as me looked healthy, but in my opinion, anyone could detect that I was not a healthy person. I looked anorexic and underfed. With a small body frame, my illness made me look even thinner, and the worry over my treatments made it difficult to follow my diet.

During my treatments, I craved raw pasta and the block form of Milk of Magnesia. I purposely wore clothing with pockets and hid those items in them. Strangely, eating while I was receiving my treatment blocked some of my fears. A nurse caught me eating, took the items I had wrapped in a napkin to her desk, and announced, "There shall be no eating in the unit."

Needless to say, I was embarrassed, not because I was caught eating but because of the items I was eating. From that day forward, the nurses monitored patients more closely. The unit nurses and doctor on duty were not familiar with that type of magnesia, so the doctor asked the intern from my native land about it, and he explained that it is the same antacid and/or laxative as the liquid magnesia, but it is compacted as a block in powder form.

Chapter 4

Making the Decision

$\mathcal{I}$n the evening, the nephrologist stopped by my room to reaffirm that I would be dialyzed again the coming Monday at 7:00 A.M. to start my routine treatments and that I would remain in the hospital until the end of my first full week of treatments. In addition, he mentioned a possible kidney transplant and said I should think about it, since it takes a lot of planning and research. He also told me that if I went in that direction, I'd need to get my name on the waiting list.

It brought up a clear question. I lay back against my pillow and thought about the two options. I could either survive on my own with less worry and visit the hospital as an outpatient to continue the dialysis treatments for God knows how long, and stay alive that way, or I could put my name on the transplant waiting list and risk going under the knife. But this could also mean a complicated, dangerous surgery and the risk of the transplanted kidney not functioning. After much thought, I felt that the transplant might be the better option, but I still wasn't ready to make the final decision.

When I told my family that I was thinking about a transplant, my mother and sister did not wait for my decision; they immediately volunteered their kidneys. My sister was underage at the time and needed my mother's approval, but neither one of them was about to procrastinate. They saw the misery I was going through and realized that my life was in jeopardy, and they wanted me to get over my illness.

When their blood was tested, the first step to determine if there was a "match" to my blood, neither one of them had my blood type, a critical requirement; therefore, they were unsuitable donors. My father had my blood type, but he was deceased.

When my relatives and extended family heard I was contemplating a new kidney, they came to the hospital in droves to be tested. They were willing and hoping to donate one of their kidneys so I could live a normal life. It was only then I realized how much they cared about my well-being, since we hardly saw each other or communicated regularly. Again, none of them had the compatible blood type. I thought deeply and my second option became the choice — going on the transplant list, even though I still could not erase the lingering doubt. The thought of getting a transplant had been too much to scrutinize, and now I wanted to rest for a while.

While en route to dialysis for my second treatment, I looked around and saw patients waiting to be dialyzed. I learned that they came in all ages — an eye opener for me. It made me aware that kidney disease is an ailment with no age limit; it doesn't discriminate, and illness is one of life's great equalizers. The youngest patient there was eight years old. As a young person myself, yet several years older, I couldn't help thinking about what could be going through the child's mind. Being attacked as a young person was both frustrating and devastating for me; it was stealing away my youth, but I considered myself lucky that I was still young and at an age when I could fight for my life.

I had difficulty coming to terms with where my life had taken me. I couldn't believe that I had come to depend on a machine or someone else's kidney to live a full life, and I still couldn't understand "Why me?" I wanted an explanation and non-medical advice, but when I listened to adults telling me to stop worrying, to stop feeling sorry for myself, and to go out more often, *I ignored their suggestions.* This wasn't their life; it was mine, and I had to do what I believed was right for *me.* I had no idea what that was, and I went back and forth looking for the "right way" to move forward. In all this, I was losing hope. I stared in the mirror and sucked my teeth constantly — a habit referred to in Barbadian vernacular as a "steupse".

When I reached my peak of frustration — losing weight and losing my taste buds, I said to myself, *"What will be, will be."* I lived by that statement and trusted in God to see me through. If He wanted me to live a long life, He would allow it, and if it were my time to go and it was His will, then there was nothing I could do about it. This attitude gave me some comfort, as it took the responsibility out of my hands. I worked harder at enjoying life in the days left to me, and I kept telling myself that life has an expiration date.

Going through this ordeal, I put up a façade, forcing myself to look happy when I came in contact with people, matching their happiness. I faked this appearance when I met people who I knew, and the longer I kept it up, the easier it became. This faux happiness helped me through a time of a sad situation. To me, faking it was making it, despite the challenges.

I couldn't help wondering what my life would have been like if I had stayed in my homeland among familiar faces and environments. Although I had no control at the time I came to the USA, I felt deep within that if I had not come, I would not have gone through my distress. However, I couldn't be sure that even if I had not immigrated, I would be well. But an irrational part of me said I had not been sick until I came here, that the chilled temperature had given me a cold, which brought about the medical attention that led to my condition. Whether this is true or not was beyond my ability to reason. My kidneys may have failed regardless of the penicillin, but it may have taken longer; yet something in my head blamed my immigration for my health issues.

I never told anyone how I felt about this. I knew my mother would feel responsible if she heard that I assumed that this had played a role in my becoming ill. She had been at my beck and call from its inception, and I imagine it would be like sending a dagger through her heart, and the last thing I would want is make her feel guilty for my affliction.

On January 2, 1976, about fifteen minutes after I arrived in the dialysis unit, the renal social worker and the dialysis head nurse approached me about signing the transplant waiting list. I was caught off guard and said, "I haven't made my final decision. I will let you know later."

I wrestled with the idea of surgery. Pessimism was in play, but part of my mind was already made up to have a transplant rather than spend the rest of my life on dialysis. However, I could not shake off the thought that kept coming before me that if the surgery went well and my body accepted the new kidney, there would still be the ongoing dangers of infection, and the new kidney might work only for a short time.

Nevertheless, the scales were tipping in favor of a transplant. My inner self told me to do it, and I followed through, but I made it known to the dialysis team that I did not want to know any of the details about the surgery — what it would be like, who the organ came from (male/female), etc. It wasn't that I preferred to be under-educated or I wasn't interested. Instead, I knew that hearing or reading anything about the surgery would cause me insomnia. Worse, my stomach cramps would return and I'd have difficulty eating properly. I needed to be as healthy as possible for the surgery, and losing sleep or weight would not be helpful.

After I gave the okay to be added to the waiting list, the social worker told me they would do whatever needed to be done, and she went off to start the process. I remember her saying, "Let's keep our fingers crossed and hope it won't be too long before you get a new kidney." This was before implementation of the computerized database called UNOS (United Network Organ Sharing) in 1977 to list candidates and to help them find matches for organs.

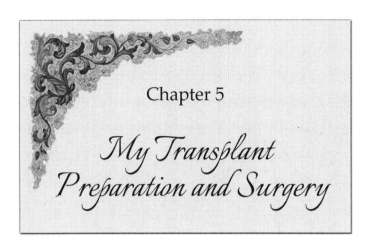

Chapter 5

My Transplant Preparation and Surgery

$\mathcal{T}$he most significant turning point in my life was on February 13, 1976, six weeks after I went on the waiting list. I received a call at work at about 2:00 P.M. from a urologist at the New England Deaconess Hospital, preparing me for what may be in sight, the gift of a new kidney. He asked me when I was last dialyzed and how I was feeling. He followed up with a few more questions and then said, "It looks like we might have a kidney; we'll get back to you." He hung up and I was happy. Then the nervousness set in, and I was left to wait and wonder.

I became more and more nervous through each passing hour, and I didn't know how I would get through the remainder of the day. I walked down three flights of stairs to the cafeteria at work and sat there to clear my head. Upon returning to my office, I called my mother at work to tell her about the call. My supervisor and co-workers did not know I was on the transplant waiting list, so I left work Friday afternoon without whispering a word to anyone, in case things did not work out. The last thing I needed was other people's disappointment on top of my own.

I went directly home, wondering if I would get a call to come to the hospital later that evening. I was on pins and needles waiting for the call. Meanwhile, a family friend stopped by unexpectedly. While chatting with her, I let her know without giving her a reason that I was awaiting a phone call and may have to leave on a moment's notice. All kinds of thoughts went through my head — *Am I about to get a new kidney? Is this for real? Will it turn out the way I want it? What will happen when I go to the hospital? How long will it take before I know for sure?* Sadly, the urologist didn't call back and I went to bed on edge and disappointed.

It was now Saturday, February 14, 1976, Valentine's Day (also known as National Donor Day). It's a day I can't forget if I wanted to. I had just finished my breakfast when the phone rang. It was the long-awaited call from the hospital telling me to get there as soon as possible. They had a kidney available, but they needed to run tests on me, and the sooner I got there, the quicker I could get through the prerequisites and get into surgery. I had been waiting and praying for this moment, and it was finally here, but I was still somewhat skeptical. Was this kidney really a match for me?

I hung up the phone, looked at my mother and sister, and told them the news. My mother had a broad smile. She went to her bedroom to change her clothes, and then she called a taxicab to take me to the hospital. I had already taken a shower, and I hurried to my room to get dressed. I gathered things to take with me — nightgowns, housecoat, toiletries, and I put them in an overnight bag.

It was a cold and windy morning. I put on my favorite coat and zipped it all the way up, wrapped a black scarf around my neck, and put on a black wool cap, pulling it down snugly over my ears for warmth. Before leaving home, my mother called her eldest sister, who lived in the apartment building next door, to tell her the news about my prospective kidney. Then she looked deep into my eyes and said, "Let's go," and we walked through the door.

Neither of us knew what to expect, but we were optimistic. As we headed out into the frigid temperature, my mother stopped by my cousin's apartment in the same building, to let him know where we were going. With my cold and shaking hands in my pockets, I tried not to think too hard about what was happening as we boarded the taxicab.

Fragments of the day stuck in my mind and made a strong memory. I realized, regardless of the day's outcome, that this was the day when my health and life would become better or worse and that even the smallest of details could prove relevant. I made a conscious choice not to get excited — this was assuming, of course, that I got the kidney. After all, there were a million ways things could go wrong. I understood there was a fifty/fifty chance for success — transplant surgery was still in its early years, far from perfect, and I viewed it as risky. Having listened to discussions among kidney patients, I came to appreciate that transplants took place fairly often, but the success rate in terms of longevity was not as encouraging as it is today.

When I arrived at the hospital, the receptionist directed me to the waiting room for blood and urine tests. I told myself that the results would indicate whether I was healthy enough for the surgery, and more importantly, whether my body would accept the kidney. After the tests were completed, a nurse escorted me to another area to wait for the results. I sat patiently, twiddled my thumbs, and glanced at my mother repeatedly, while she stood by the door waiting anxiously to hear if I would go to surgery. She wore a worried expression on her face, and it occurred to me that the wait must be as difficult for her as it was for me.

I was still uptight about what I envisioned to be an "experimental surgery". Still not knowing what to expect, my mind wandered, confusing me. I was unsure whether to go through a long and complicated surgery, with the hopes of walking out of the hospital with a new kidney, or to forego the surgery and walk out just as I came in — with deteriorating kidneys, and face the prospect of an on-going life with ill health and frequent dialysis appointments.

I waited for what felt like hours. I could not remember blood and urine results taking so long. *Did they forget I'm here? Did something go wrong? Are they trying to delay giving me bad news?* With those thoughts, I prepared myself to return home without a new kidney. I mustered the strength and energy, took a deep breath, and pushed down the disappointment. I focused on the thought that it would only happen if it was the right time and if God was willing.

Suddenly, a urologist I didn't know came striding into the room and looked straight at me with a smile, "Things look good, Ms. Blades. Your surgery is scheduled for two this afternoon."

I asked, "Does my doctor know? Is he on duty?"

"I haven't seen him, but I'll check," replied the urologist. I heard my doctor being paged, and within a short time he came to see me and assured me everything would be fine and not to worry. He told me that another patient I knew who was dialyzed at the same time was also there to be tested for a new kidney, and with a twinkle in his eye, he added, "Maybe the two of you will wave at each other in the recovery room."

At 1:45 P.M., a nurse and an IV technician entered the room simultaneously. The nurse told me they were ready for me and she gave me a gown to put on. The IV technician set up an intravenous drip — a liquid dripping into a vein, a drop at a time — via a tube and needle inserted into the skin. Before I could blink twice, an orderly came to the room and told me he was there to take me to the OR. I climbed onto the stretcher with tears running down my cheeks.

My mother rubbed and kissed my forehead, and we waved to each other as I was wheeled away. Many thoughts flashed across my mind — *I'm getting a kidney from someone who is dying or has died. Will I be free from dialysis? Is this the answer to my prayers?* I quickly cut those thoughts off, not wanting to put too much pressure on myself.

The anesthesiologist greeted me with a smile as I entered the OR; he was friendly and witty. It was extremely cold inside the room, and I was shivering. Being nervous, I did not want to delay an inch of time. I wanted to have the surgery done as soon and as quickly as possible. When I could not tolerate the cold any longer, I told the anesthesiologist I was freezing. He left and came back with several blankets, placing one after the other over my shoulders and chest, with my arms neatly tucked underneath. One of the doctors there reassured me that everything would be fine and they would take care of me. He told me I was tiny and they would be finished with the surgery in no time. I asked him where Dr. X was, who I had been told was going to do the surgery.

He responded, "He's out getting chicken feed, but he will be here shortly." I did not see him; another doctor completed the procedure. I don't know where he really was — maybe he had some hungry chickens.

The anesthesiologist standing there told me that he was going to numb from my waist down so I wouldn't feel anything. I later learned that it was an epidural anesthesia. As I glanced over, somewhat groggy, I saw some bright, silver objects to my right, and I immediately said, "Put me to sleep." I saw him inject something into one of the intravenous lines. The process was about to get started and I heard, "Count backwards, starting with ten."

I started, "Ten, nine, eight . . ." and then there was blackness.

Before I knew it, I was awake again. A nurse standing beside my bed explained, "You're in the recovery room now." The surgery was over.

The surgeon came by to check on me, and he said a few words I couldn't understand. I mumbled at him through a fog of lingering anesthesia and then fell back to sleep. When I woke up again, I was in the ICU. Now it was a question of whether the new kidney would survive.

Chapter 6

My Recovery

$\mathcal{I}$ had a new kidney, and I was hoping to live a long and healthy life. The next morning, when I opened my eyes, my mother and my aunt were standing over me. My eyes were cloudy and I couldn't see them clearly, but I could hear their voices. I was worried about my vision and whispered to them, "I cannot see your faces."

I recall hearing my aunt telling my mother, "Patty's skin tone has darkened. Did you notice it?"

My mother responded, "I'll get the nurse to call the doctor." In the meantime, my aunt fainted but quickly regained consciousness. With everything going on, I never found out why my skin looked darker.

Within a few minutes, my nephrologist walked into the room, "You went into surgery talking and came out talking."

I could hear him smiling through the words. "How do you know?" I asked.

"It was on your chart," he answered.

"I was nervous," I replied. Then I said to him, "I can't see clearly. My eyes are cloudy." "There you go worrying again. They will clear up."

Then he said that everything had gone well and that I should have a quick recovery. I took him at his word and felt relieved that it was over.

The first time the nurse came to measure my urine, there was a large amount in the plastic bag, something I hadn't seen for a long time. I discovered that my new kidney was positioned to the lower front left of my abdomen, while my native kidneys were still in their positions. This is the norm. They don't remove the old kidneys in a transplant unless it is determined they would cause a problem.

My first day in ICU flew by quickly. I was hungry around lunchtime, but there was no lunch tray for me, so one of the nurses took a tray from the cart. She removed the packets of salt and said to me, "Eat something."

On Monday morning, following my surgery, I asked my mother to call my supervisor to inform her of my whereabouts.

Unknown to me, my kidney did not function right away, but the transplant team was optimistic. The second day, they cast worried glances in my direction — my body was rejecting the kidney.

I said, "Oh no! Are you going to take me back to the operating room?"

"No surgery," they told me. "We'll work on it from here."

I felt let down. I had to face those washing machines again. An orderly came and took me in a wheelchair to the dialysis unit to clean my blood and stimulate the new kidney in an attempt to increase its function. In addition, the surgeon scheduled me for four radiation treatments starting the following day. After my second dialysis treatment, the head nurse of the unit came to my room and told me that if I put out a certain amount of urine every twenty-four hour period, my dialysis treatments would be discontinued.

The only way I knew to accomplish this unreasonable request was to force myself to drink lots of water, which I disliked with a passion. I was sad and uptight, dreading the treatments to open up the kidney and make me urinate more, but I drank until I felt as if my stomach would burst. A nurse measured my urine every two hours. The morning of my third treatment, I waited anxiously to go and get it over with, but no one came to take me. I called the nurses' station to let them know I hadn't been picked up.

Within half an hour, the dialysis head nurse came to my room. She smiled and said, "Do you think we forgot you? Your output has improved. It's been good, so we'll hold off your treatment today."

I was delighted. I felt a smile forming. For the first time in six years, I was as happy as a pig in mud. From that day forward, after my second radiation treatment, the kidney opened up and functioned normally and the remaining radiation treatments were canceled. I continued to drink as much water as I could to keep my kidney functioning and to prevent having to resume dialysis.

The incision was healing so well that a few days after surgery the surgeon removed the surgical drain. I was pleased and thought it meant I would be going home soon. So far, there had been no complications except the first rejection, which was under control, and all signs pointed to my body accepting the new organ.

After spending close to a week in the ICU, I went to a private room on another floor where precautionary measures were taken to protect my frail body. Visitors and hospital staff wore a gown and mask when they entered the room to limit my exposure to germs. I saw constant improvement in myself while recuperating. The kidney was functioning as it should, and I continued to force myself to drink plenty of water to keep hydrated. I urinated frequently and felt that I was on the rebound. By the end of the second week, I built up my hopes that I would be going home by the end of the next week.

Strangely, I experienced another setback. I was having pain around the area of my incision. It felt as though a heavy object was resting to the front lower left side of my abdomen. I have a high tolerance for pain, so I kept quiet about the discomfort and did not mention it to the nursing staff. It was the only problem I was experiencing, and I thought there might be a range of different and harmless reasons for it — I probably should have mentioned it.

One day, when I went to the bathroom, the incision burst opened and yellow, foul-smelling pus seeped out. I returned to the bed and called the nurse. Meanwhile, the nephrologist walked in. I told him of the incident and the seepage, and he examined me. He ran his hand over and around the incision. He mentioned that the area was warm, and when he pressed around it, the incision oozed, but I had no signs of a fever. He immediately called the surgeon, but he was in the OR. My pending release had been within sight until that moment, and I realized that my dreams of being discharged in two weeks were shattered.

When the surgeon came to the room, he looked at the incision and said there was no time to prep me for the OR. He stepped outside, and within a few minutes three nurses entered. One of them was pushing a cart with several wrapped items and a five-gallon bottle of clear liquid that looked like water. He instructed one of the nurses to hold one of my hands and another nurse to hold the other hand. He asked the nurse that pushed the cart to put the pump on the bottle while he unwrapped a piece of medical equipment shaped like scissors. Before I could say anything, he punched the incision with the instrument, spreading the sides of the wound, and then he pumped water in to flush it out. It was painful, and I screamed and struggled against the nurses holding my hands.

I recall one of them saying, "You can swear if you want."

I noticed the other nurse standing next to the wall, looking as though it was as painful for her as it was for me. This was one of the most excruciating things I had ever experienced — it seemed as though every procedure I now faced was worse than the last one. The surgeon did not close the wound with stitches; he left it open, maybe to prevent any further infections. When he and the nurses left the room, I put my head on the pillow, exhausted by the pain, and fell asleep.

Every other day, the surgeon came to examine the incision by poking it to make sure it was healing from the inside. I dreaded his visits and closed my eyes as if I were asleep as soon as I saw his shadow entering the room. I hoped that if he thought I was asleep he would turn away, but he never did.

While I was recuperating, I had several blood transfusions. The first one caused an allergic reaction, mainly itching all over my body, hives on my face, and I tried to pull out my hair to get some relief from the sensation. The nurse stopped the transfusion and sent the blood to the lab. The test results revealed that the cells in the blood caused the allergic reaction. Henceforth, the label on the plastic bags for my transfusion read, "With washed cells."

I spent a total of four discouraging weeks in the hospital — one day for surgery and the remaining time for recovery. Finally, the day came when I was set free. My body was responding to the kidney, and I was already making great strides in my physical health. When I had been admitted, I weighed a scant 73 pounds. Upon my discharge, I weighed 112 pounds, and my pants were two sizes too small, but my body was supporting itself and I was ready to start a new life. My illness had been a long process. I traveled the longest, most twisted route. Eventually, I was on my way home and this was all that mattered to me.

Chapter 7

Alive

*W*hen I was discharged, the doctor gave me two prescriptions: Prednisone, which I had been taking for a while, and Imuran, an anti-rejection medication. He also gave me instructions on how to take care of the incision and an appointment to visit the surgeon (urologist) at the Lahey Clinic twice a week to make sure the incision continued to heal as it should. He cautioned me to be very careful, to stay away from people with colds and the flu, as any shocks to my system or preventable illnesses could endanger the precious kidney.

It was not an easy time for me because the prescribed medications had serious side effects. I developed several unusual symptoms: My appetite increased tremendously as did my bloating, and I developed a "moon face" from the steroids. I ate as if food was going out of style and it was my last meal. Prednisone had a role to play in the swelling and in my weight gain. During the first two years of taking it at a very high dosage, my weight quickly reached 156 pounds, which was far too heavy for my small frame. I was self-conscious and unhappy about gaining weight, but I wasn't sure how to combat this effect. The doctor gradually adjusted my dosage. I also cut back on my food intake, and by the end of the third year, my weight had decreased and was in proportion to my height and body frame.

Life didn't wait for me to get back on my feet. When I arrived home from the hospital, the phone was ringing. My mother answered. It was the acting supervisor at my job who was covering for the supervisor. To my surprise, I heard my mother say, "My daughter did not just have her tonsils removed." She shook her head in disbelief and gave me the phone. The supervisor told me she had called the hospital and was informed that I had been discharged earlier that day, and she was calling to find out when I would return to work.

My doctor and I had not discussed returning to work, so I was unprepared to answer her question. I told her about my follow-up visit with the surgeon in two days and assured her that I would let her know as soon as my doctor gave me the all clear to return. I was not aware that there were limitations on the number of days an employee could be absent without a penalty.

A few days after our conversation, I received a letter in the mail from the employer stating that my health benefits were about to be canceled due to my lengthy absence — the four weeks I had been hospitalized. Attached to the letter was a pink form to fill out if I opted to pay my out-of-pocket monthly health premiums. I was flabbergasted when I received the form, but I filled it out and paid my own premiums until I returned to work full-time.

The Sunday following my release from the hospital, I still had quite a bit of soreness from the incision frequently being poked and cleaned, although it *was* healing. I had hoped that my sickness was over, but I wasn't willing to go on the road to recovery by myself. I needed God's help and the support of my fellow believers. Despite my discomfort, I decided that the first thing in resuming my life was to go to church, that it was time to renew my faith for the continuing journey.

I got up early, took a shower, ate breakfast, and then got dressed in a new outfit my mother bought me after she saw that the clothes I'd once worn to church were now too small. The two of us boarded the streetcar, and I stood up all the way during the entire ride to the last station a few yards away from the church. I hurt — but persevered. When I got to church, I saw people whom I hadn't seen in months. They were surprised to see me at church so soon after my discharge, and I could tell from the smiles on their faces that they were happy to see me. I was overwhelmed and pleasantly surprised by the many people I had never met who knew my story and welcomed me back.

The kidney was adapting to my body and doing its own work, but at the same time, the medications harmed other parts of my body. Prednisone came with a range of side effects, and I experienced more emotional highs and lows than I ever had before. I felt that I should mention it to my doctor. At one of my follow-up visits, I asked him how long I would have to take the medications. His response was discouraging. He said that I would have to take both medications for the rest of my life.

My heart sank. This certainly was not what I wanted to hear.

However, he told me that eventually the dosage would decrease as the kidney took to my body and required less support. In hindsight, the infected incision may have been caused by the Prednisone, which I had been taking prior to surgery, and it may have been what slowed down the internal healing process.

As years went by, I continued to develop more side effects from the two medications. However, I kept telling myself that the side effects were a small price to pay for a healthy kidney. I had the privilege to travel longer distances without fear of getting sick, and I was finally free to eat anything I desired.

I encountered and continued to deal with several minor health issues, including the removal of cataracts from both eyes. Warts grow on my arms, which caused me to stop wearing sleeveless clothing. I developed osteoporosis and still continue to take a calcium supplement with Vitamin D daily and a prescribed medication to aid with my bone loss. My skin bruises easily. I still visit the dermatologist annually to keep abreast of my skin lesions and possible skin cancer. I still have constant mood swings. I have hypertension and take a calcium channel blocker to decrease my blood pressure, and I take a beta blocker to slow my heart rate.

About two years post-transplant, my blood pressure had stabilized within normal range, so I stopped taking the medication. At a follow-up visit, the doctor asked if I needed a refill, and I told him that I had stopped taking it. He asked who had taken me off. I responded, "Dr. Blades," my last name.

He looked at me somewhat surprised and said, "I didn't know there was a doctor in your family."

Looking directly at him with my chin lifted high, I said, "Dr. X, you are looking at her. I have no reason to continue taking it if my blood pressure is under control."

He shook his head and smiled as if to say he could not believe what he was hearing. He wrote a prescription and told me to continue taking it. I obeyed his orders.

When I returned to work, my co-workers and supervisor gave me a warm welcome. They were happy to see me, and they were surprised at my weight gain and how healthy I looked. They asked who had donated the kidney, and if it was from a man or a woman, and how close the match was. I did not know nor had I thought to ask after the procedure, since I hadn't wanted to know the details beforehand. It was the furthest thing from my mind, and to me it was not important. But the constant questioning made me curious — *Who has saved my life? Is there someone I should thank?*

"I thought you didn't want to know anything," my doctor joked when I asked him. "Are you standing or squatting when you go to pee?"

I stared at him, slightly confused by his comment. He quickly changed the subject and I did not persist. Yet, it did not take me long to catch on to his wittiness that the donor had been a woman. I suspected that his wit had led him to make this leap; however, in my ongoing conversations with him, he never shared information about the donor or the condition of the kidney. This type of information was not disclosed in those early years.

The fistula clotted a few months after my discharge. I did not need to use it, but I had mixed feelings about removing it. I felt that if I ever needed dialysis, it would be available for quick access, but on the other hand, it had become a useless object. I consulted with my nephrologist about it, and he wasn't keen on having it removed since it wasn't causing me any problems. I was pleased with his viewpoint, especially knowing I didn't have to go through the pain and frustration of surgery again. Anything that meant avoiding surgery was music to my ears.

About fifteen years post-transplant, I believed that the kidney had established itself. I asked my former nephrologist about discontinuing the Prednisone and Imuran or switching to other medications due to the damage they did to me.

His response was the same as before, a resounding, "No! *If it's not broken, why try to fix it? It's easier to control a side-effect and adjust medications than to be on dialysis or find a matching kidney."*

I wondered if his response was based on the kidney being from a deceased unrelated donor or if it were a reaction from the "old school" of medicine. But the more I thought about his response, the more sense it made and I accepted his rationale. Lastly, I didn't want to go through another surgery or transplant any more than he wanted. Given the side effects of the medications and knowing there is no cure for my medical condition, I was always grateful, although they caused me stress.

When my new nephrologist came on board, he too was not in favor of discontinuing the medications, and he didn't believe changing them was a valid option. The two of them presumed that it would present a risk to the transplanted kidney. Eventually, I found my own peace with their logic, and I stopped asking about trying other medications.

I learned at a kidney seminar that a deceased-donor kidney transplant lasts about ten to fourteen years, but the lifespan depends on many factors, such as how healthy the new kidney is at the time of transplant, the recipient's health, and whether they are following a diet that is based on the amount of intake more so than the food itself. To me, it meant that my kidney could last longer if I took care of it — and that was paramount.

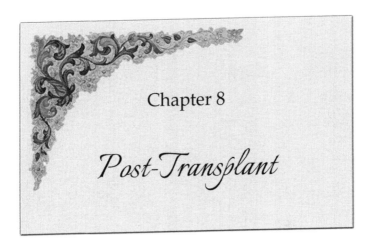

Chapter 8

Post-Transplant

From the inception of my illness, the thought of dying never crossed my mind, even with all the pain and suffering I was going through. I was not as strong in my faith then as I am today, but I had a desire to make it through my illness. To think of dying in a strange land when I had so much to live for was unacceptable. I did whatever I had to — before and after the transplant — to keep my feet in the land of the living.

My mother's friends came by, especially on weekends, and sometimes stayed overnight, praying for my recovery and giving me support. I attended many faith-healing crusades to boost my emotional energy and to ask for additional prayers. The crusade I remember best is that of Katherine Kuhlman, an evangelist who was a noted "faith healer". I was amazed at the large turnout at her crusades, and people with various ailments claimed they were healed at previous gatherings.

I was determined to live the "good life" that I had long dreamed of, and I told myself, *Now is the time.* I was given a fairly clean bill of health and could go places and do things that had been curtailed, and I felt renewed. I spent my youth wanting to do great things with my life, but I left that thought behind when I fought to live from one day to the next. The time came when I could pick up where I left off. I pursued the educational goals and career aspirations I had discontinued when I became ill.

I love crunching numbers and spent many years in the accounting field. While at home recuperating and looking back at how my sickness started, I found it mind boggling and fascinating to see how blood and other medical tests could pinpoint an illness. The more I thought about it, the more interested I became. I considered a career change and researched specific medical careers, but I was most attracted to laboratory science. I believed that such an education would help me learn more about my condition and be able to help myself while I helped others — It seemed like a perfect idea.

I enrolled in a Medical Laboratory Technician program the next year after my surgery and attended evening classes while I worked full-time. I received a certificate as a Laboratory Assistant at completion nine months later — a proud moment of my life. I saw this accomplishment as a sign that I was moving forward in every sense of the word, and it became a banner of my belief.

I encountered many twists and turns during my entire ordeal. During some periods, I wondered if my unpleasant situation would ever end. My friends and family never seemed to lose faith and did not allow me to give up. They gave me the motivation to get through my illness, to pursue a productive life, and they picked me up when I needed it.

Four months after my transplant, I returned to my full-time job in the communications industry, but due to my suppressed immune system, I waited six months after the surgery to work as a part-time phlebotomist and laboratory assistant. My body wasn't strong enough to defend itself against any illnesses or medical challenges I might have run into, and I wouldn't take any chances with my health until I was sure I could handle it. I was protective of my new kidney and wanted to avoid any setbacks. I hadn't done research on kidney transplants, and I didn't know if direct contact with infectious patients could harm my new kidney. For that reason, I was apprehensive and decided to quit the phlebotomy and lab work a few weeks later.

I spent more time with my family and friends in spite of my crowded work and school schedule. I did things I hadn't done in years that healthy and energetic people do, things that were previously restricted to me. I took lengthy trips instead of the short, tense trips I used to take, and I didn't have to worry about dialysis treatments. I was glad when I got the okay from my doctor that I could travel to my birth country of Barbados. I could dine with friends more often without the fear of my intake and leave home without the fear of becoming ill. My first night out to a restaurant was the joy of ordering the dessert — rum and raisin ice cream.

I treated my medication like the American Express mantra: "Don't leave home without it," and I found that it was a safeguard for me. Going through renal failure, dialysis, and transplantation placed a different outlook on my life, and things eventually became brighter, bigger, and more meaningful to me.

I retired after twenty-five years of working in different departments at the telecommunications company and spent some of my time giving back to the community. I co-founded a Caribbean non-profit organization in Massachusetts that teaches children of Caribbean descent about their culture and heritage through steel pan music. I offered my help occasionally at the church I attended and other organizations. I volunteered particularly during kidney month (March); it gave me an opportunity to meet people from all walks of life who knew of a family member or friend with a kidney disease. During some of my spare time, I learned how to needlepoint and macramé, but I also crocheted, knitted, baked, wrote skits, and shared those passions with friends, family, and people I did not know. Most of all, I enjoy Gospel music and hymns, and I love to sing from this genre. I share my compassion with people I meet who think they might become a donor or recipient.

Some may see these things as insignificant, but to wake up to the radio, put your feet on the floor, and make a cup of coffee was, and still is, a blessing to me. I never stopped being thankful, and I never stopped seeing every day as a new beginning. I will never forget that I was close to death and was brought back to life by the competence of urologists, nephrologists, and one noteworthy, memorable donor.

Chapter 9

Life Today

*M*any things changed for me after the transplant, and I have made several important transitions in my new life. Things are not always as easy and carefree as I would like, but there are reasons for the new rules, and I do what I have to do to keep myself healthy. For the past several years, I have been enjoying many foods that I had not eaten in years, but I continue to be conscientious with my intake. Pre-transplant, I stayed away from salt, and to this day, I do not use added salt in my diet and avoid foods high in sodium. About twenty-five years after the surgery, I started to eat lightly-salted foods such as potato chips, lightly-salted peanuts, and other low-sodium items that offer a safer less-salty option. I enjoy the milder, more subtle flavors of less-spicy foods, and I continue to use much of my pre-transplant diet except for the salt-free bread and the salt substitute. I remember vividly my mother cooking with salt-free spices. I rated them to be worse than bland food and boldly hid them from her.

Being on Prednisone, I watch my sugar intake, knowing it can cause high blood-glucose levels. Foods I loved pre-dialysis and still do to this day, to name a few, are: cheddar cheese, Cadbury chocolate, popcorn, soft serve ice-cream, and some of the Caribbean baked items, but I use smaller portions and less frequently, and I savor every bite as though it was my last.

I presume that the longevity of my kidney is partially due to the care I've given it in terms of my diet. Although not required, I monitor my intake so that the kidney doesn't have to work too hard, and I forgo foods that might stress the kidney too much. It has lasted years longer than the average life span for an unrelated donated kidney and maybe for this reason. According to the *New England Journal of Medicine*, a kidney transplant from a deceased donor now lasts an average of twenty years. I've doubled those years!

Several years ago, the results of my routine blood tests were alarming, and my nephrologist referred me to a hematologist who ordered extensive tests. The results showed hair-raising numbers. The hematologist explained that for the amount of time I was on Imuran — an immunosuppressant to prevent rejection — it could have caused some numbers to escalate and others to decrease, and this contributed to the results.

I was upset when I heard the hematologist's diagnosis and went to my nephrologist's office to relay the findings. He said I may need another transplant — this time bone marrow. The hematologist wanted to see if any internal damage was done, and if so, how much. He scheduled a bone-marrow biopsy for the following week, which is a test I would not wish on my worst enemy.

Luckily for me, the results of the biopsy were negative. He requested that I make an appointment to see him in six months. Eventually, my blood results returned to normal, but it was unclear what really contributed to those earlier results.

Since my transplant, I have had two exploratory surgeries — an appendectomy and a hysterectomy; both are stand-alone stories.

I had been battling hypertension with numbers reaching close to 300 over nearly 200, and it was described as "malignant". I had relocated to another state, so I went to a doctor there. He kept changing the blood pressure medications, but none of them were effective. One of them stopped me from urinating. I quickly flew back to Massachusetts and went directly to Urgent Care at the Lahey Clinic where I had been an outpatient over the years. I was transferred to the Emergency Unit and was diagnosed with acute renal failure, and I spent three days in the hospital.

During an annual physical, I was hospitalized again for extremely high blood pressure. It was scarier than the previous hospitalization three years earlier. The blood pressure medication wasn't working, so the nephrologist wrote a new prescription to fill at the on-site pharmacy and to take immediately. He requested that I return to his office within two hours. My blood pressure showed no signs of reduction. Because of my allergies, he researched other medications and gave me a prescription for yet another medication.

I returned to see him the next day. The pressure had come down but was not close to normal, so he told me to continue with the medication and scheduled an appointment to see him two months later.

During that night, I realized that I had not urinated since early morning. I kept trying and I could not. I started to think of my first bout in 1969 that led to renal failure. Early in the morning, I was scheduled to return home. Instead, I canceled my flight and returned to the hospital.

Upon arrival, I learned that the Urgent Care Unit did not open until 5:00 P.M., so I called the doctor's office, but he was not in at the time. However, he instructed his secretary to order certain tests before he saw me later that day.

When I met with him, my pressure was more than double the normal range on both the top and bottom readings, and the results from the tests showed acute renal failure. He said it was hard to determine at the time if my escalated blood pressure had caused the kidney to react or vice versa. I was more concerned about my kidney and having a rejection than I had been about my high blood pressure numbers. Nonetheless, I was admitted under the care of Internal Medicine.

I spent a total of eight days in the hospital, as well as my thirty-fifth transplant anniversary. I did not have any symptoms such as blurred vision, headaches, dizziness, etc., that indicated my blood pressure numbers were high. It's no wonder it is called, "The silent killer."

While I was in the hospital, the medical staff had a difficult time selecting the appropriate medications that would lower my numbers without affecting the kidney and causing allergic reactions. With the trial of different medications mostly given intravenously, my heart rate started to drop rapidly to the point where there was immediate concern to focus on my heart. At one point, I thought I would lose consciousness from the different procedures performed. However, after several hours, my heart rate improved.

Finally, on the sixth day, after taking medications intravenously and orally, my blood pressure finally started to stabilize, although it was still far from normal, but my heart rate was under control. Thinking that I was on my way to recovery and had one foot out the door, I found out one of the new oral medications increased my creatinine level, and my kidney was not functioning as it should. However, a doctor told me that the team was watching it closely.

I said, "Here we go again! Medications are good and bad!"

Luckily for me, I did not have to take any additional medications, and my kidney returned to its normal functionality within two days.

Doctors were amazed that my *CAT (CT) Scan*, the equipment that provides detailed, cross-sectional views of my brain, as well as the results of other tests, showed no signs of a stroke, heart attack, or some other kind of serious damage to my body, other than the acute renal failure. The doctors told me that my blood pressure will never be normal — 120/80.

The day I was discharged, my pressure was in the 170s over the high 80s. When I saw my nephrologist, he jokingly said to me, "You are a complicated patient."

I responded, "Isn't that the story of my life?"

Epilogue

*I*t would be an understatement to say that my young adult life was turned upside down and many scars were left on it. Some of my memories are bittersweet and some painful; some I try to forget, as they bring me bad dreams.

At the onset of my illness, I was in a state of denial, filled with fear, and I did not want to know anything about the disease. My attitude was to let the medical professionals do whatever they thought was necessary without giving me the details. As years went by, I understood that my illness was not simply acute; it was at the chronic stage. At this turning point, it was too important for me to leave it up to other people. After my transplant, I become very interested in my health and eager to learn about the causes and effects. I realized that I couldn't educate myself if I didn't ask questions and keep myself informed. For the last twenty-five years, I have become vigilant in seeking knowledge, and I am now my own best advocate.

After receiving my new kidney, I became the most jovial, light-hearted person you've ever met. I built the confidence to speak at a kidney conference, and on other occasions to tell people about my journey with kidney disease. Today, I am a transformed person; I have been lucky to have superb specialists — nephrologists and urologists.

My initial nephrologist — soft spoken and kind, yet firm with his orders — is now retired. Sometimes he gave me latitude in terms of not adhering to my appointment dates, but it was not too often. I sat in his office on many visits, and we talked about any and everything — his family, local and national news, etc. I talked with him about other medical concerns or personal issues, and he was always willing to listen and was never in a hurry. I met his replacement around the same time, when I was initially admitted to the hospital for observation. He is also now retired and pleasant but not a talker. My current nephrologist is a replica of my initial doctor, only much younger. I have been lucky to have doctors who are never too busy to add me to their already busy schedule and have helped to save my life on multiple occasions.

I have been privileged to have a deceased non-relative kidney transplant, and fortunate that it has lasted forty-plus years and counting. Since 1970, I have been an in/out patient at the Lahey Clinic in Massachusetts, which at the time was affiliated with the New England Deaconess Hospital, where my initial diagnosis with kidney disease and my transplant surgery was done.

During the past three years, I have lab work done annually in the state where I now live, and I visit the Lahey Clinic every year to have a complete physical. I keep a watchful eye on my test results that are critical to my kidney function: creatinine and BUN (blood urea nitrogen). I watch my cholesterol and monitor my glucose daily. I am happy to report that the only kidney problems I have had since the second day after the transplant were the two times mentioned above when I was prescribed new medications for my blood pressure and they caused acute renal failure.

As I get older, I think and worry about potential new side effects and my kidney being rejected. I cannot entertain thoughts about going back to dialysis. My sister reminds me that *it's no use worrying about something I can't control, and I've turned to the Serenity prayer. "God grant me the serenity to accept the things I cannot change; courage to change the things I can, and wisdom to know the difference." This prayer has given me a way to take my mind off the worries.*

My transplant has caused me to put a different value on my daily experiences and has given me the opportunity to improve my life and my family's life, which could not have happened otherwise. The mere thought of going through the changing scenes of my life, compounded by the many hurdles I encountered, and to think how blessed I am, and how far I've come literally, all make me realize that my faith and the miracle of organ transplantation have been my sources of strength.

Although every day is Thanksgiving for me, the holiday has gained special significance. It is the holiday that marked the memory that stands out the most. Every year, since my transplant, I fast on Thanksgiving Day, beginning on Thursday morning and ending Friday morning. It's my own thanksgiving and my promise to God and myself that I will continue living my life being thankful for every day.

Surviving these many years is miraculous. My journey continues to be a success, and I remind myself each day that my success has been a journey. This journey taught me, "Backward never; forward ever," and not to look back but to continue climbing those rungs. Having a foreign kidney in my body is more significant than I ever could have imagined. It gave me hope and helped me move forward so I could experience life fully as a normal person.

It was through the unselfish act of organ donation by an unknown person and his or her family that I received the utmost second chance of life and was given the opportunity to tell my story. Each day, I acknowledge the "gift that keeps on giving" and celebrate the "gift of life." I appreciate and extend my sincere gratitude to the unknown person and the family who made the donation possible. Their identities are unknown to me but not forgotten. The memory of this kind gesture will stay with me for as long as I live. Through it all, I regret that during my early years of receiving the kidney, information about the donor's family was not disclosed. I never met them, although it is possible they didn't want to know who received their loved one's organs.

Nevertheless, I would have liked to say thanks. I use every day of life to thank them.

Obviously, my story is of the medical world as it existed nearly a half century ago. Medicine has come a long way since my disease, and outcomes have improved significantly over the years. It would be unrealistic to compare my experience forty years ago to what a kidney patient may undergo today. Anti-rejection medications were limited then and weren't available if patients had medication allergies or experienced side effects. This restricted the choices for people such as myself who couldn't take most of the available medications.

In this era, there are myriad new medications to protect transplanted organs from rejection, with far fewer side effects than I and other patients endured in the past. There are many alternative medications to provide choices in case the initial medication stops working or starts to negatively impact kidney function. The amount of medication used in this day and age is reduced dramatically, compared to what transplant patients took several years ago. For instance, Prednisone is tapered down, and even eliminated, sometimes by the time a patient is released after the transplant, or at most a few months later. Some of the techniques have changed and surgeries have become more routine and less complicated.

While much is the same, there has been so much advancement in today's world to make this particular procedure quicker than it was when I experienced it.

Beyond that, the average time to leave the hospital after surgery can be quite different for every patient. There are countless twists, turns, and obstacles for each of us on that journey. Keep in mind that no patient goes through exactly the same process. This is my unique story; hopefully yours is much better.

Transplanted Kidney

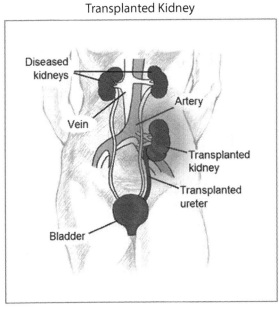

This diagram was taken from an article about Sir Michael Woodruff, an English surgeon and scientist who researched organ transplantation.

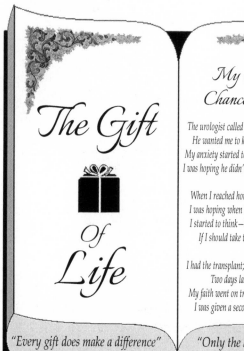

The Gift

Of Life

My Second Chance at Life

The urologist called at work, it was the day before
He wanted me to know what might be in store
My anxiety started to build, I was filled with fright
I was hoping he didn't call in the middle of the night

»»«««

When I reached home I stood close to the phone
I was hoping when he called I wouldn't be alone
I started to think—hmmm—I wasn't quite sure
If I should take the risk or should I forego

»»«««

I had the transplant; I didn't know what to expect
Two days later my kidney rejects
My faith went on trial and God saw me through
I was given a second chance to live life anew

"Every gift does make a difference"   "Only the living needs a kidney"

Acknowledgments

*M*y journey has been filled with stress, fear, heartbreak, pain, and some danger, and I would not have made it so far without the help of some of the people in my life. I offer special and heartfelt thanks to my mother, who was by my side whenever I needed her and spent many sleepless nights by my bedside. She watched me when I grappled with pain and fear and held my hand through the course. I would also like to thank my sister, who has been there for me whenever I needed her.

I would like to express my appreciation and extend sincere thanks to my relatives and close friends, who took time out of their busy schedules to offer prayers, encouragement, and support during my illness; the medical and surgical staff at the New England Deaconess Hospital, who took part in my transplant; my former nephrologists, who were available whenever I contacted them, and the medical staff at Lahey Clinic, who continue to follow up with my aftercare.

I would also like to say thanks to my friends at MDJunction, PatientsLikeMe, the Transplant Café websites, and my real-world friends — all of whom encouraged me to tell my story.

I extend gratitude to Jim Gleason, a heart transplant recipient, for allowing me to share with my readers the movies from his library (See Appendix - "List of Kidney/Organ Transplant Movies" on page 129.) Jim is the author of the book, *A Gift from the Heart*, and has graciously shared his story and thoughts with many people. If you're interested in learning more, please see his movies and story at: http://www.rjwitte.com/changeofheart/Gift.

Last but not least, I would like to thank my editor for helping me express myself more fully and *HelpPublish.com* for assisting me with the cover design, the book layout, and for guiding me through the publishing phase to share my story in print and electronically.

About the Author

*P*atsy Blades was born and raised on the Caribbean Island of Barbados and migrated to Boston, Massachusetts, in 1969. Within a few months, she was stricken with kidney disease, went through dialysis, and received a kidney transplant. She now resides in Orlando, Florida. This year was her 41st anniversary of a deceased unrelated donor kidney transplant. The author can be contacted at vze2tf8u@gmail.com.

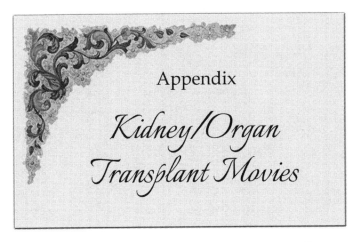

Appendix

Kidney/Organ Transplant Movies

L = A DVD or VHS movie physically in the library collection.
V = Jim has viewed this movie.
S = This feature has been shown in our quarterly Transplant
    Movie Night series.

13 Moons – Comedy

A crazy group tries to find a kidney donor for their friend's son, happening upon a drunk who seems to fit the bill. They have trouble keeping him in the hospital.

Beats, Rhymes & Life – Hip-Hop Documentary

A documentary about a Hip-Hop group tribe called Quest. Included as a small part of the storyline, one of the rappers receives a kidney transplant from his mother.

D tour (L, V) – True-Life Self Documentary

A professional musician's dream of being in a successful Rock 'n' Roll band comes true. But just as his band starts to take off, his kidney starts to fail. *D tour* is a Rock 'n' Roll film that chronicles the life of this musician with no "back-up plan" as he is faced with daily dialysis, a grueling tour, and a search for a new kidney.

Derailed – Drama

After saving money for years for their diabetic daughter who needs a kidney transplant and a new expensive experimental medication, the husband gets into an affair that gets complicated, involving a robbery and rape and so much more out-of-control action.

Dying to Live (L) – Documentary (2010)

Tracing stories of three transplant candidates, doctors, and other medical experts, as well as sharing insightful advice and dispelling common myths. This is a great film for anyone thinking of becoming an organ donor.

Final Sale – Action Drama (Lifetime TV movie)

An illegal kidney transplant recipient learns that her donor died in the operation and takes on a crusade to stop such practices.

Gift of Love (L, V, S) – True-Life Family Love Story

Based on a true story, *Gift of Love* tells the story of a high school student, Daniel Huffman, who looks to have a promising future in football. He is very close to his grandmother who helped to raise him and who is in desperate need of a kidney transplant. Daniel selflessly gives her one of his, a choice that results in him never being able to play football again.

Nicholas' Gift (L, V) – Family Docudrama

A fact-based drama about an American couple on vacation in Italy in 1994 with their two children and are attacked and shot by highway bandits. This results in their son being brain dead. The parents are then faced with the hard decision to donate the boy's organs, which ultimately leads to saving the lives of seven seriously-ill Italian patients. When controversy arises over the religious implications of organ transplant in Italy, only through the Green's incredible charity does the country see the true blessing of Nicholas' gift! An inspiring story that touches the whole world!

No Greater Gift (L) – Family Drama

Two terminally-ill boys strike up a friendship in a hospital ward. One of the boys with a brain tumor decides to make the ultimate sacrifice, a kidney donation to the other, so he can have a chance at life.

No Greater Love – Educational Video (60 min)

A PBS documentary funded by the U.S. Department of Health and Human Services (HHS), created to raise Americans' awareness about the need for organ and tissue donors, shows the healing that may come through the act of donation. It follows several families, health care providers, and recipients to weave together an emotional and dramatic depiction of organ donation and transplantation in action.

Pour toujours, les Canadiens! – Sports Story, Family Friendly

Built around the making of a movie about the very real event, the hundredth anniversary of the Montreal Canadiens, this story is about a ten-year-old boy awaiting a life-saving kidney transplant and how he gets to meet his heroes, the hockey team of the film.

Race Against Time – Sci-Fi Thriller Drama

Facing surmounting bills for his dying son's hospital stay, a father enters into an agreement to sell his body for organ transplants to pay the bills. When he is advised that the doctors want to claim his organs immediately, he goes on the run.

Seven Pounds – (L, V, S) Drama, Romance

An IRS agent tries to redeem an unforgivable mistake he made in the past by helping seven people. Spoiler: The transplant movie of all transplant movies.

Sympathy for Mr. Vengeance – Horror Drama

A young deaf-mute man's failed plot to obtain a kidney for his ailing sister sets in motion a chain of events ending in a series of vengeful murders and black-market organ trafficking.

The Details – Comedy

A Black Comedy about a living donor kidney story, as well as many others!

The Donor (L) – Drama

A stuntman picks up a beautiful girl in a local bar, takes her to a motel, and wakes up the next morning with one of his kidneys missing! He takes off on a manhunt to find who did this to him. (Note: The book of the same title is good reading too.)

The Indian (L) – Family Drama

A touching drama about a negligent father who must face the son he abandoned years earlier and the emotional wreckage he caused in order to obtain a life-saving kidney transplant.

The Kindness of Strangers (L, V) – Documentary

A feature-length documentary; this is an intimate journey into the lives of people confronted with organ donation and transplantation.

The Ultimate Gift (L, V) – Romantic Comedy/ Family Drama

When his wealthy grandfather dies, trust fund baby Jason Stevens anticipates a big inheritance. Instead, his grandfather has devised a crash course on life: twelve tasks or "gifts" designed to challenge Jason in improbable ways, sending him on a journey of self-discovery and forcing him to determine what is most important in life: money or happiness. Along the way, this story just mentions that his late father is a living kidney donor (That is not developed in the story.) to his life-long lawyer friend, but the young girl who befriends Jason is a bone marrow transplant recipient needing another transplant, and that develops in an inspiring way throughout this movie.

Trick Dribble (L, V, S) – Teen Drama

Good basketball dribbling show, but the too-short transplant story is missed if you blink.

Yolanda King, daughter of Dr. Martin Luther King Jr., plays two roles in this action-packed movie about the mother of a college basketball player who uses his skills to win the money to pay for his mother with serious kidney disease needing a kidney transplant soon in order to save her life.

White Men Can't Dance – Family Drama

A family's grandpa dies in their arms while waiting for a surgeon. When their little girl becomes deathly sick and needs $50,000 for a kidney transplant, the father calls his old dance buddies to get back into shape to compete in a break dancing competition to save his daughter's life.

44975758R00087

Made in the USA
Middletown, DE
21 June 2017